RECORD BREAKERS!

Penguin
Random
House

Senior editors Chris Hawkes, Scarlett O'Hara, Fleur Star
US editor Jennette ElNaggar
Senior designer Sheila Collins
Designer Kit Lane
Design assistance David Ball
Illustrators Adam Benton; Stuart Jackson-Carter;
Jon @ KJA Artists; Simon Mumford; Peter Bull;
Nigel Wright @ XAB Design; Dynamo Ltd; Square Egg
Creative retouching Steve Crozier
Picture research Sakshi Saluja

Jacket designer Surabhi Wadhwa-Gandhi
Jacket design development manager
Sophia M Tampakopoulos Turner
Jacket designer Juhi Sheth
DTP designer Rakesh Kumar
Jackets editorial coordinator Priyanka Sharma
Managing jackets editor Saloni Singh

Producer (pre-production) David Almond
Senior producer Angela Graef

Managing art editor Philip Letsu
Managing editor Francesca Baines
Publisher Andrew Macintyre
Art director Phil Ormerod
Associate publishing director Liz Wheeler
Publishing director Jonathan Metcalf

First American Edition, 2018
Published in the United States by DK Publishing
345 Hudson Street, New York, New York 10014

A catalog record for this book
is available from the Library of Congress
ISBN: 978-1-4654-7438-4

DK books are available at special discounts
when purchased in bulk for sales promotions,
premiums, fund-raising, or educational use.
For details, contact: DK Publishing Special
Markets, 345 Hudson Street, New York,
New York 10014
SpecialSales@dk.com

Printed in China
A WORLD OF IDEAS:
SEE ALL THERE IS TO KNOW

www.dk.com

RECORD BREAKERS!

CONTENTS

Planet Earth

People power

Sporting prowess

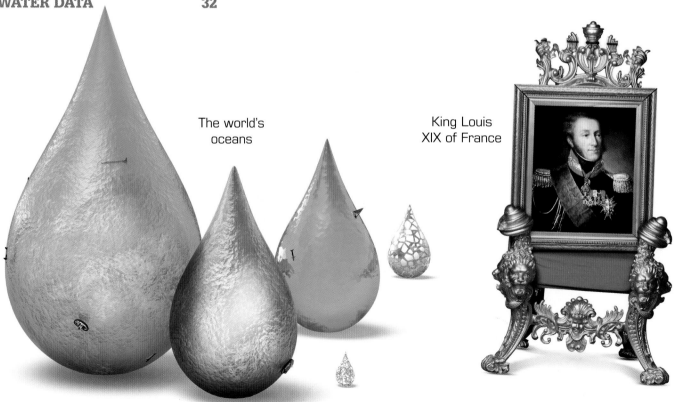

The world's oceans

King Louis XIX of France

Feats of engineering

Living world

Out of this world

Capybara

Baluchistan pygmy jerboa

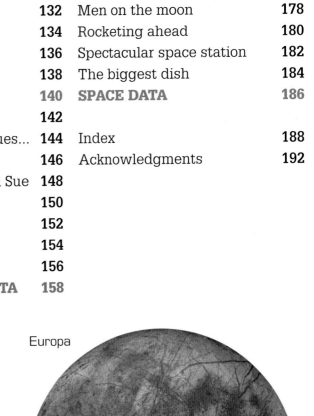

Europa

Planet Earth

Nature is always the star of the show in planet Earth's most dazzling displays. From electric storms and erupting volcanoes to swirling tornadoes and spectacular seas, this record-breaking trip around the world shows nature in all its glory.

Electrifying lightning strikes light up the sky over Lake Maracaibo, Venezuela, on an average of 260 days of the year. There are about 640 lightning flashes per sq mile (250 per sq km) here—that's a higher density than anywhere else on Earth. On some nights, the lake sees more than 1,000 strikes an hour.

Where on Earth?

Our planet is amazing! Most of the time, it has just the **right conditions for life**. Some places, however, are very, very hot, really wet, or **incredibly snowy**.

Earth's landscapes vary hugely, ranging from rugged mountain peaks to dry salt flats and from icy polar deserts to baked volcanic terrain. Here are some of the most extreme places on our planet.

Flattest place
The flattest area on Earth is the world's largest salt flat, Salar de Uyuni, in Bolivia. It covers a vast area measuring 4,050 sq miles (10,500 sq km).

FAST FACTS

The strongest-ever earthquake occurred on May 22, 1960, in Valdivia, Chile. The earthquake had a magnitude of 9.5.

The largest impact crater on Earth measures 186 miles (380 km) across and was made by an asteroid. It is at Vredefort, South Africa.

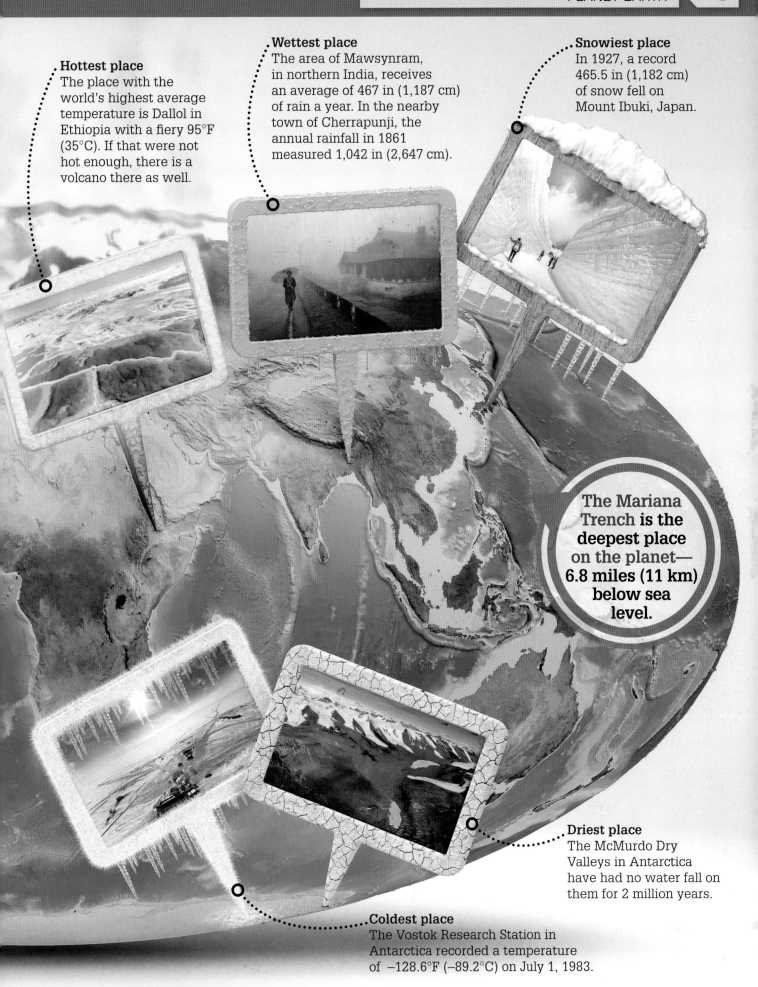

Hottest place
The place with the world's highest average temperature is Dallol in Ethiopia with a fiery 95°F (35°C). If that were not hot enough, there is a volcano there as well.

Wettest place
The area of Mawsynram, in northern India, receives an average of 467 in (1,187 cm) of rain a year. In the nearby town of Cherrapunji, the annual rainfall in 1861 measured 1,042 in (2,647 cm).

Snowiest place
In 1927, a record 465.5 in (1,182 cm) of snow fell on Mount Ibuki, Japan.

The Mariana Trench is the deepest place on the planet— 6.8 miles (11 km) below sea level.

Driest place
The McMurdo Dry Valleys in Antarctica have had no water fall on them for 2 million years.

Coldest place
The Vostok Research Station in Antarctica recorded a temperature of −128.6°F (−89.2°C) on July 1, 1983.

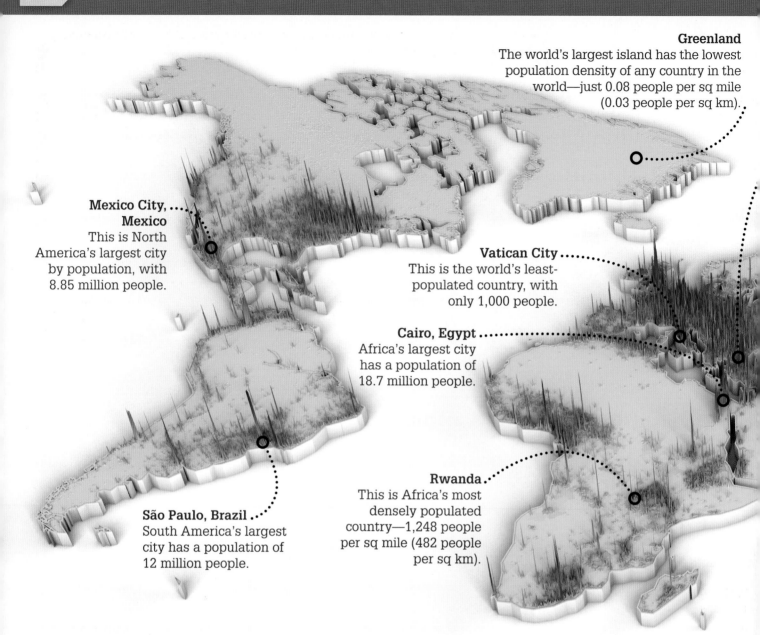

Greenland
The world's largest island has the lowest population density of any country in the world—just 0.08 people per sq mile (0.03 people per sq km).

Mexico City, Mexico
This is North America's largest city by population, with 8.85 million people.

Vatican City
This is the world's least-populated country, with only 1,000 people.

Cairo, Egypt
Africa's largest city has a population of 18.7 million people.

São Paulo, Brazil
South America's largest city has a population of 12 million people.

Rwanda
This is Africa's most densely populated country—1,248 people per sq mile (482 people per sq km).

Where does everybody live?

The **world's population** is estimated to be **7.405 billion**. But which are the **most densely populated countries** on Earth, and where are each continent's **most-populous cities**?

PACKED TOGETHER

Macau, a Special Administrative Region of China, is the most densely populated country on Earth. It has a population of 648,500, with 59,500 people per sq mile (22,998 people per sq km).

Istanbul, Turkey
With a population of 14.7 million people, this city is considered the largest in Europe, even though it has a foot in both Europe and Asia.

This map shows where people live on Earth.
The height of each spike represents the number of people who live in a particular area. Southeast Asia, the Indian subcontinent, and northern Europe are the world's most densely populated areas.

India
This country has the world's second-largest population (1.281 billion people) but is expected to become the world's most-populous country by 2028.

China
The world's most-populous country is home to 1.379 billion people—approximately one-fifth of the world's population.

Shanghai, China
More people live inside this city's boundaries (24.3 million) than in any other city on Earth.

Java
Forming part of Indonesia, this is the world's most-populous island, with a population of 139.4 million people.

Sydney, Australia
The largest city in Australasia and Oceania, it has a population of 4.9 million people.

Almost **two-thirds** of the **world's population live** in **Asia**.

MEGA CITY

Located on the Yangtze River Delta on China's northeastern coast, Shanghai is a major global financial center and home to the world's busiest container port. It also has more people living within its city boundaries than any other city in the world—a mind-blowing 24.3 million people.

While volcanic eruptions can be deadly, sometimes the aftereffects cause more problems. Large ash clouds have blocked out the sun, changing the weather and causing starvation through harvest failures.

Loudest eruption
Krakatoa's 1883 eruption was the loudest noise ever recorded on Earth. It could be heard 3,100 miles (5,000 km) away.

Longest eruption
Mount Stromboli, on Stromboli island, Italy, has been continually erupting for at least 2,700 years.

Most deadly
When Tambora, Indonesia, exploded in 1815, 70,000 people died, largely from the crop failure that followed.

Violent volcanoes

Rock-shattering **explosions**, burning **lava**, choking **ash clouds**... All volcanoes are **dangerous**, but which are the most **extreme** of all?

Of the world's **1,500** potentially active volcanoes, **20** are erupting **at any one time**.

Largest eruption
Mount Toba erupted about 75,000 years ago in an explosion 100 times bigger than Tambora in 1815. It spewed out about 672 cubic miles (2,800 cubic km) of debris.

Fastest lava flow
Mount Nyiragongo, in the Democratic Republic of Congo, has the largest lava lake, which in 1977 caused the fastest lava flow: 40 mph (60 km/h).

FAST FACTS

The countries with the most volcanoes are the US (173) and Russia (166). They are both large countries, but the main reason they have so many volcanoes is because they touch the "Ring of Fire." This is an imaginary line around the Pacific Ocean where most volcanoes occur. The line also goes through Indonesia, Japan, and Chile.

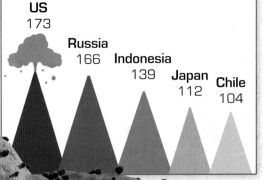

US
173

Russia
166

Indonesia
139

Japan
112

Chile
104

What a gem!

Here is a collection of some of the world's most precious **gemstones**. Some are **very valuable** because they are so huge; others are **rare** and have been **elegantly cut** to bring out their beauty.

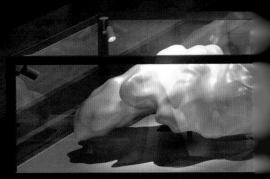

Largest pearl ever found
A fisherman in the Philippines discovered this giant pearl weighing 75 lb (34 kg) in 2006. It is thought to have come from a giant clam.

World's most expensive gemstone
A beautiful pink star diamond was sold at auction in 2017 for a staggering $71.2 million (£57.3 million). This very high-quality stone weighs 59.6 carats.

World's largest blue star sapphire
This egg-shaped gem was found in Sri Lanka in 2015. When a light is shone on it, a six-sided star appears. It weighs 1,404.49 carats and is named the Star of Adam.

Biggest opal in the world
This giant piece of opal came from a mine in south Australia in 1956. It was named Olympic Australis and weighs 17,000 carats.

Biggest gold nugget
Called the Welcome Stranger, this nugget was discovered by two miners in Victoria, Australia, in 1869. It weighs 145 lb (66 kg).

Largest cut diamond in the world
A huge yellow stone called the Golden Jubilee was found in a diamond mine in South Africa in 1985. It was cut into a sparkling gem weighing 545.67 carats.

FAST FACTS

Gemstones are usually weighed in carats. One carat is roughly equivalent to the weight of a drop of water. Some gigantic gems weigh the same as some birds or small animals.

1 carat 0.007 oz (0.2 g)		A drop of water
50 carats 0.3 oz (10 g)		Two hummingbirds
100 carats 0.7 oz (20 g)		Barn swallow
1,000 carats 7 oz (200 g)		American red squirrel
5,000 carats 35 oz (1,000 g)		Black-footed ferret
10,000 carats 70 oz (2,000 g)		Ring-tailed lemur

Twister!

Spinning along the ground at up to **70 mph** (110 km/h) and reaching up to the **clouds**, a strong **tornado sucks up** whatever lies in its path, causing **devastation**.

A tornado forms when warm, moist air near the ground meets cool, dry air above, making the warm air rise up in a spinning column. Large tornadoes can rotate as quickly as 300 mph (480 km/h), be 2.6 miles (4 km) wide, and last for 30 minutes while tearing across the landscape and destroying anything in their path.

Fastest wind
During a 1999 tornado in Oklahoma, wind speeds inside the funnel reached 301 mph (484 km/h) at 330 ft (100 m) above the ground.

Oklahoma City

STORM-CHASING

The dangerous pastime of storm chasing involves tracking and following storms and hurricanes to photograph them. American David Hoadley is credited as the pioneer of storm chasing. He started in 1956 and has seen more than 230 tornadoes.

Deadliest tornado
In Bangladesh in April 1989, the Daulatpur-Saturia tornado destroyed trees and houses over 2.3 sq miles (6 sq km), killing 1,300 people and injuring thousands more.

The longest tornado lasted **3.5 hours** and **traveled 218 miles** (352 km) through **three states** in 1925.

Longest distance carried by a tornado
A tornado that struck Missouri, USA, on March 12, 2006, swept up a trailer with Matt Suter inside. It was carried 1,307 ft (398 m) before it came down, but Matt survived.

Most tornadoes
In 2011, a "super outbreak" of tornadoes hit 21 states and parts of southern Canada. In total, there were 362 tornadoes over 72 hours, causing damage worth $11 billion (£7.9 billion).

Widest tornado path
In 2013, the El Reno tornado carved a path through Oklahoma 2.6 miles (4.2 km) wide—officially the widest on record.

Hottest desert
Sahara

The highest land temperature ever recorded was in North Africa's Sahara Desert—136°F (57.7°C) at El Azizia, Libya, on September 22, 1922.

Driest desert
Atacama

Some weather stations across the Atacama Desert, in Chile, have never recorded a drop of rain. The average rainfall across the desert is 0.6 in (15 mm) per year.

Largest sand desert
Rub' al Khali

Also known as the Empty Quarter, the Rub' al Khali, which forms part of the Arabian Desert, is the largest continuous sand desert in the world.

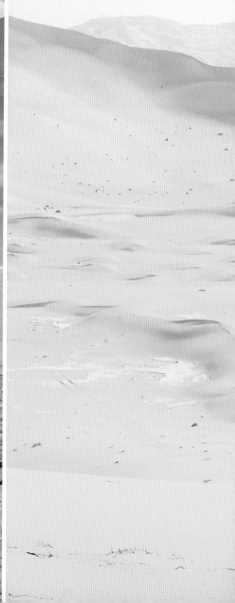

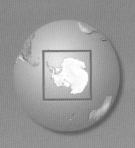

Biggest desert
Antarctica

The Antarctic Desert is the world's largest. It covers 5.5 million sq miles (14.2 million sq km) and is more than one-and--a-half times the size of the Sahara Desert.

Oldest desert
Namib

Having endured arid conditions for 55 to 80 million years, southern Africa's Namib Desert is thought to be the oldest in the world.

Deserts

A **desert** is a place that receives **less than 10 in (25 cm) of rain** per year. But not all deserts are hot. The **world's largest desert** is found in freezing **Antarctica**.

Deserts can be found on every one of the world's continents and cover more than one-fifth of land on Earth. Surprisingly, only 10 percent of the world's deserts are covered by sand.

AN OCEAN OF SAND

The Rub' al Khali, also known as the "Empty Quarter," is the largest area of continuous sand in the world. Forming part of the Arabian Desert, it covers 250,000 sq miles (650,000 sq km)—an area larger than France, Germany, and Spain combined.

Mountain high

Mount Everest may well be the highest mountain in the world, but there are plenty of other record-breaking peaks out there.

From rockfalls to hypothermia, there are many risks associated with climbing mountains—and not just the taller peaks. Mont Blanc, on the border of France and Italy, may be only 15,780 ft (4,810 m) high but has still claimed the lives of 8,000 mountaineers and hikers.

Deadliest mountain to climb
Annapurna, Nepal, is the world's 10th highest mountain. Fewer than 200 people have climbed it successfully, with one in three climbers dying in the attempt.

Highest unclimbed mountain
Gangkhar Puensum, Bhutan, remains unclimbed despite several attempts. And it looks set to remain so, as in 1994 all mountains in Bhutan over 19,685 ft (6,000 m) were closed to climbers, to respect local spiritual beliefs

Annapurna
26,545 ft (8,091 m)

Gangkhar Puensum
24,836 ft (7,570 m)

It is likely that Gangkhar Puensum, Bhutan, will never be summited.

Most climbed mountain
Every year during July and August (the official climbing season), a staggering 300,000 people climb the 12,389-ft (3,776-m) Mount Fuji, near Tokyo, Japan.

Mount Fuji (3,776 m)
12,389 ft

Highest cafeteria in the world
Rinchen Cafeteria sits 18,380 ft (5,602 m) above sea level on the Khardung Pass, on the Indian side of the Himalayas.

Highest cafeteria in the world

FAST FACTS

The "seven summits" are the highest mountains on each continental plate. Everest is nearly 6,562 ft (2,000 m) taller than the next highest, Aconcagua. Although Puncak Jaya is in Indonesia, it is situated on the Australian continental plate.

Everest, Asia
29,029 ft (8,848 m)

Aconcagua, S. America
22,838 ft (6,961 m)

Denali, N. America
20,321 ft (6,194 m)

Kilimanjaro, Africa
19,340 ft (5,895 m)

Elbrus, Europe
18,510 ft (5,642 m)

Vinson, Antarctica
16,050 ft (4,892 m)

Puncak Jaya, Indonesia
16,024 ft (4,884 m)

Copper mine
The mine is thought to have produced more copper than any other mine in history, as much as 19 million tons (17.2 million tonnes).

Empire State Building
The towering Empire State Building in New York is 1,250 ft (381 m) tall. This means it would take two and a half of them to reach the top of the mine.

This vast open-pit mine is the largest man-made excavation on Earth. The mining of copper began here in 1906, and now the mine covers 1,900 acres (770 ha), which is equivalent to the size of a small town.

What a massive mine!

Bingham Canyon mine, Utah, is a **massive crater** 3,182 ft (970 m) deep and more than **2.5 miles (4 km) wide**. The mine produces **copper**, gold, silver, and a metal called molybdenum.

In 2013, the mine suffered North America's largest nonvolcanic landslide.

Mining vehicles
This tiny speck is actually a huge excavator digging out the stepped sides of the pit.

📊 FAST FACTS

These are the deepest excavations on Earth compared to the deepest undersea trench and the highest mountain.

The deepest man-made hole is the Kola Superdeep Borehole, Russia. Begun in 1970, it reached 7.6 miles (12.3 km) deep by 1989.

AngloGold Ashanti's Mponeng gold mine in South Africa is the world's deepest mine.

The deepest ice core (2.2 miles/3.6 km) was drilled out at the Vostok Research station, East Antarctica.

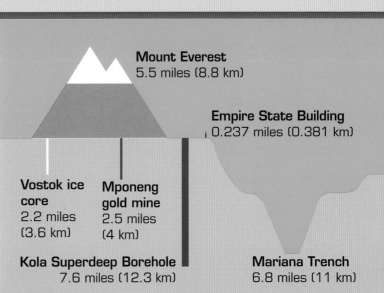

Mount Everest
5.5 miles (8.8 km)

Empire State Building
0.237 miles (0.381 km)

Vostok ice core
2.2 miles (3.6 km)

Mponeng gold mine
2.5 miles (4 km)

Kola Superdeep Borehole
7.6 miles (12.3 km)

Mariana Trench
6.8 miles (11 km)

Watery world

Earth is a **blue planet**, with more than **two-thirds** of the surface covered in **water**. These **oceans** contain **97 percent** of all our **water**. Dive in to discover the oceans **making waves** around the world.

The five named oceans are the Pacific, Atlantic, Indian, Southern, and Arctic. They are all connected around the seven continents, so in reality there is only one great ocean covering our world.

Pacific Ocean

SHRINKING SEA

The Aral Sea (actually a freshwater lake in central Asia) was once the fourth-largest lake in the world, but it is shrinking fast. In 2014, its eastern basin (seen to the right of the image) dried up for what is thought to be the first time in 600 years.

160,700,000 cubic miles (669,880,000 cubic km)

The record-breaking Pacific is easily the biggest ocean, holding more than half of the world's seawater. All of Earth's continents could fit comfortably inside the Pacific Basin. It is also the deepest ocean. What's more, about 75 percent of the world's volcanoes are found beneath its waters.

The Pacific Ocean contains more water than all the other oceans combined.

FAST FACTS

The deepest parts of the oceans are shown in this chart. The Mariana Trench, in the Pacific, is the deepest point on Earth: if Mount Everest was dropped inside, its summit would still be more than 1 mile (2 km) below the ocean surface.

Depth in feet					
7,000					
13,000	Mariana Trench, Pacific: 36,070 ft (10,994 m)	Puerto Rico Trench, Atlantic: 28,374 ft (8,648 m)	Java Trench, Indian: 25,344 ft (7,725 m)	South Sandwich Trench, Southern: 23,740 ft (7,236 m)	Litke Deep, Arctic: 17,881 ft (5,450 m)
20,000					
26,000					
33,000					
39,000					

Atlantic Ocean

74,470,000 cubic miles (310,410,900 cubic km)

Coming second to the Pacific, the Atlantic is the next largest ocean and also the saltiest sea. These bountiful waters are known for gas, oil, and fish. The Atlantic widens by up to 4 in (10 cm) every year as the continental plates beneath its surface move farther apart.

Indian Ocean

63,337,000 cubic miles (264,000,000 cubic km)

More people live on the shores of the Indian Ocean than any other ocean. About one-fifth of the global population have set up home here, enjoying the world's warmest waters where the temperature can reach 82°F (28°C).

Southern Ocean

17,225,600 cubic miles (71,800,000 cubic km)

Surrounding icy Antarctica, the Southern Ocean was considered an extension of the bigger oceans until it was officially given its name in 2000.

Arctic Ocean

4,500,000 cubic miles (18,750,000 cubic km)

Just a drop in the ocean compared to the others, the Arctic Ocean is the smallest and shallowest, and also has the least salty waters.

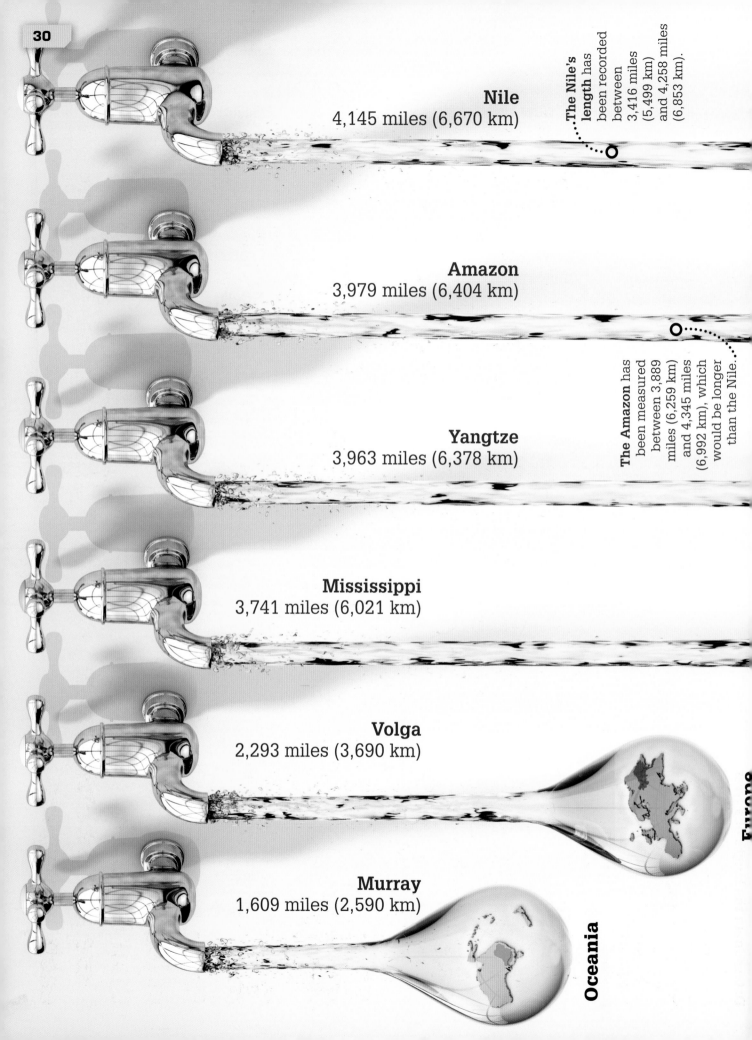

Nile
4,145 miles (6,670 km)

The Nile's length has been recorded between 3,416 miles (5,499 km) and 4,258 miles (6,853 km).

Amazon
3,979 miles (6,404 km)

The Amazon has been measured between 3,889 miles (6,259 km) and 4,345 miles (6,992 km), which would be longer than the Nile.

Yangtze
3,963 miles (6,378 km)

Mississippi
3,741 miles (6,021 km)

Volga
2,293 miles (3,690 km)

Europe

Murray
1,609 miles (2,590 km)

Oceania

Record rivers

Earth has **countless** rivers, with at least **165 major rivers** longer than 621 miles (1,000 km). Here are the **longest** on each **continent**.

Determining the length of a river is not easy. There may be different results depending on which tributaries are included and where you measure from—not every river has a clear source (start) or mouth (end). Because of this, there is much debate about whether the Amazon is actually longer than the Nile.

There are no permanent rivers in Antarctica.

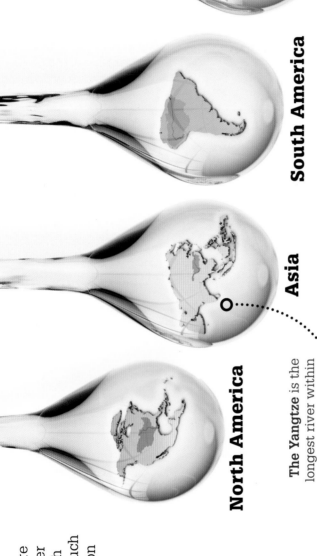

North America

Asia

The **Yangtze** is the longest river within one country (China).

South America

Africa

FAST FACTS

The Amazon is the widest river (6.8 miles/11 km) and also the biggest by volume. This chart shows each continent's biggest river (the one that discharges the most water per second into the ocean).

St. Lawrence (North America)
3.7 million gallons (17 million liters)

Volga (Europe)
1.8 million gallons (8 million liters)

Fly (Oceania)
1.3 million gallons (6 million liters)

Amazon (South America)
46 million gallons (209 million liters)

Ganges (Asia)
8.3 million gallons (38 million liters)

Congo (Africa)
9 million gallons (41 million liters)

Water data

The **salinity**, or **saltiness, of water** is measured in **"parts per thousand" (ppt)**—that is, how many grams of salt there are in **1,000 g of water.** It is also expressed as a percentage, so **Gaet'ale Pond** has a salinity of **43.3 percent.**

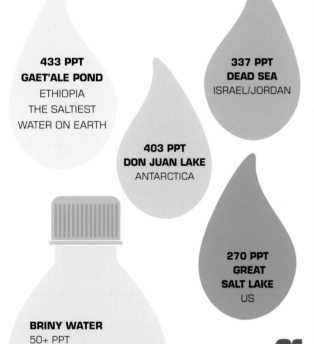

433 PPT
GAET'ALE POND
ETHIOPIA
THE SALTIEST
WATER ON EARTH

403 PPT
DON JUAN LAKE
ANTARCTICA

337 PPT
DEAD SEA
ISRAEL/JORDAN

270 PPT
GREAT
SALT LAKE
US

BRINY WATER
50+ PPT

SALINE WATER
30 PPT

38 PPT
MEDITERRANEAN
SEA

35 PPT
PACIFIC AND
ATLANTIC
OCEANS

2 PPT
LIMIT ALLOWED
FOR WATERING
CROPS

BRACKISH WATER
0.5 PPT

0.1 PPT
DRINKING WATER

FRESH WATER
0 PPT

SALTIEST **WATER**

TALLEST **WATERFALLS**

The **world's tallest waterfall is under water!** Lying in the **DENMARK STRAIT** between **GREENLAND** and **ICELAND**, the **DENMARK CATARACT** is more than **three and a half times taller** than **ANGEL FALLS**, the tallest waterfall on land.

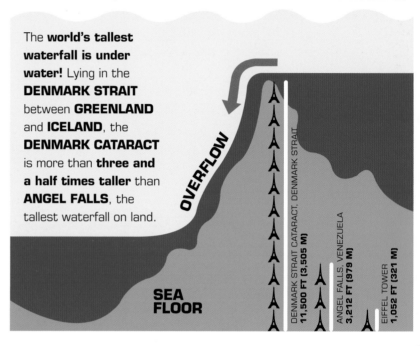

OVERFLOW

SEA FLOOR

DENMARK STRAIT CATARACT, DENMARK STRAIT
11,500 FT (3,505 M)

ANGEL FALLS, VENEZUELA
3,212 FT (979 M)

EIFFEL TOWER
1,052 FT (321 M)

DEEPEST LAKE

Although **Lake Baikal** is the **seventh-largest** lake by area, it is so deep it **holds one-fifth** of all the unfrozen fresh water in the world: **5,700 cu miles (23,600 cu km). Baikal** is on average **2,487 ft (758 m)** deep. But at its **deepest,** it sinks to **5,387 ft (1,642 m)** —that's as deep as two Burj Khalifas.

LAKE BAIKAL—AVERAGE DEPTH
2,487 FT (758 M)

BURJ KHALIFA—2,717 FT (828 M)

RAINY **RÉUNION**

Several **tropical cyclones** have set different records for rainfall on **Réunion Island** in the Indian Ocean.

DENISE, JANUARY 1966—45 IN (114.4 CM) **12 HRS**

DENISE, JANUARY 1966—71.9 IN (182.5 CM) **12 HRS**

(UNNAMED CYCLONE), APRIL 1958—97 IN (246.7 CM) **12 HRS**

GAMEDE, FEBRUARY 2007—154.6 IN (393 CM) **12 HRS**

HYACINTHE, JANUARY 1980—239.5 IN (608 CM) **12 DAYS**

3.5 TIMES THE HEIGHT OF AN AVERAGE PERSON

SATELLITE IMAGERY in use since **1970** has revealed the **most** hurricane-hit countries in **THE WORLD**: **China**, the **Philippines**, **Japan**, **Mexico**, and the **USA**.

WILD **WATERSPOUTS**

A COLUMN OF CLOUD-FILLED WIND WHIRLING OVER WATER IS CALLED A WATERSPOUT.

WATER DOESN'T SWIRL UP FROM THE OCEAN BELOW BUT DOWN FROM THE CLOUDS ABOVE.

MOST ARE SMALL, AROUND 165 FT (50 M) IN DIAMETER, AND LAST FOR JUST A FEW MINUTES.

THE BIGGEST CAN BE UP TO 330 FT (100 M) IN DIAMETER AND LAST UP TO AN HOUR.

LARGEST LAKE
PER CONTINENT

WATER **SPEED**

Running alongside the coast of the **US**, the **Gulf Stream**—a current in the **North Atlantic Ocean**—flows at **4 mph (6.4 km/h)**. Sound slow? It's still **300 times faster** than the **Amazon River's** flow rate.

These are the **biggest lakes** on each continent, by **surface area**.

CASPIAN SEA (ASIA) 143,000 SQ MILES (371,000 SQ KM)

LAKE SUPERIOR (NORTH AMERICA) 31,700 SQ MILES (82,100 SQ KM)

LAKE VICTORIA (AFRICA) 26,590 SQ MILES (68,870 SQ KM)

LAKE LADOGA (EUROPE) 7,000 SQ MILES (18,130 SQ KM)

LAKE VOSTOK (ANTARTICA) 4,800 SQ MILES (12,500 SQ KM)

LAKE EYRE (OCEANIA) 3,670 SQ MILES (9,500 SQ KM)

LAKE TITICACA (SOUTH AMERICA) 3,232 SQ MILES (8,372 SQ KM)

People power

Today, planet Earth is home to more than 7 billion people. Those that stand out from the crowd challenge themselves by relentlessly pursuing their dreams. Trailblazers strive to make history, adventurers explore unchartered territory, and leaders rule entire nations.

American Jordan Romero was 13 years, 10 months, and 10 days old when he reached the summit of Mount Everest on May 22, 2010. In doing so, he became the youngest person in history to climb the world's highest mountain. In December 2011, he went on to become the youngest to climb each of the seven summits—the highest peaks on each continental plate.

Longest-ruling royal house

Akihito is the current emperor of Japan. He is 125th in line from the first emperor, Jimmu, whose ascension is officially dated at 660 BCE. This means the same royal house has ruled Japan for more than 2,600 years!

Shortest-reigning monarch

Blink and you could miss the reign of Louis Antoine of France! In 1830, he took the French throne as King Louis XIX but abdicated 20 minutes later.

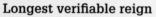

Longest verifiable reign

Sobhuza II reigned as king of Swaziland for 82 years and 254 days. After his father died, he became monarch at four months old in 1899 and remained king until his own death in 1982.

From kings and queens to prime ministers and presidents, the most memorable leaders are usually those who served their countries the longest or took charge during challenging periods of conflict and change.

📊 FAST FACTS

The longest-serving US president was Franklin D. Roosevelt, who took charge for 4,422 days from 1933 to 1945, and remains the only US president to serve three full terms.

The shortest-serving US president was William Henry Harrison who died of pneumonia in 1841, just 31 days after his inauguration.

Longest-reigning monarch today

Queen Elizabeth II has been on the British throne since 1952, making her the current world's longest-serving monarch.

First female head of state
Sirimavo Bandaranaike became the world's first female head of state when her party, the Sri Lanka Freedom Party, won the Sri Lankan elections in July 1960.

Longest-serving female head of state
Vigdis Finnbogadóttir was president of Iceland for a record-breaking 16 years from August 1, 1980, to 1996—a record for a female head of state.

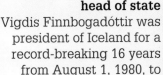

Longest-reigning nonroyal leader since 1900
Ancient leaders may have served for longer, but the modern-day winner is Fidel Castro. The Cuban prime minister and president served for 52 years and 62 days, from 1959 until 2011.

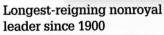

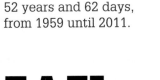

More than 70 women have become prime ministers and presidents since 1960.

Who's in charge?

From the **longest-reigning monarch** to the **first female head of state**, please stand up for the **royal rulers** and **powerhouse politicians** who have led their nations into the history books.

Film premieres

From the moment the Lumière brothers **first** presented a projected **motion picture** to a paying public in Paris on December 28, 1895, **films** have become a major form of **social entertainment**.

MILLION-DOLLAR LADY

In 1911, Mary Pickford became the first actor or actress in history to receive a million-dollar contract in Hollywood. The Canadian-born actress starred in 52 feature films.

Avatar, the science-fiction film released in 2009, is said to be the most expensive film of all time. It cost $425 million (£305 million) to make.

Jaws, director Steven Spielberg's 1974 movie about a man-eating shark, was the first film in history to make more than $1 million (£718,000) at the box office.

Since 1900, an average of 2,577 films have been produced around the world every year. The majority receive little or no attention, but others, such as the ones featured here, have made their way into the record books.

Gone with the Wind, released in 1934, is the highest-grossing film of all time. It has made $3.44 billion (£2.47 billion).

Three films hold the record for winning the most Oscars (11): *Ben Hur* (1959); *Titanic* (1997); and *Lord of the Rings: The Return of the King* (2003).

Sinbad: Legend of the Seven Seas (2003) is thought to have made the biggest loss in movie history—$163 million (£117 million).

The funeral scene in the epic historical film *Gandhi* (1982) featured a record-breaking 300,000 extras.

India produces more films than any other country in the world. In 2017, it produced 1,986 films. Nigeria lies second in the list (with 997), followed by the United States (791).

Indian film actor **Brahmanandam Kanneganti** has appeared in **1,100 films.**

Read all about it

Around 2.21 million **books** are published throughout the world each year, but which book has sold more than any other, who are the bestselling authors of all time, and which have been the world's most successful comics?

Bestselling series

The Harry Potter series of books

J.K. Rowling's series of books about a young wizard has sold 510 million copies.

Bestselling regularly updated book
Xinhua Dictionary

First published in 1957, this Chinese dictionary has sold around 400 million copies.

Bestselling cookbook

Betty Crocker's Cookbook

First published in 1950, more than 75 million copies of this American cookbook have been sold.

Bestselling authors

William Shakespeare
Agatha Christie

Two English authors, playwright William Shakespeare (1564–1616) and crime writer Agatha Christie (1890–1976, right), are both thought to have sold an estimated minimum of 2 billion books. They were both prolific writers: Shakespeare wrote 37 plays, while Christie penned 78 books.

Everyone loves a **good book**, so find a seat and browse through these **record-breaking classics**.

Bestselling nonfiction book

The *Bible*

Figures are impossible to verify, but it is thought that around 5 billion copies of the *Bible* have been sold.

Most translated author

Agatha Christie

According to UNESCO, there have been an astonishing 7,236 translations of Agatha Christie's books—more than any author in history.

Most expensive book ever sold

Book of Mormon

A Mormon church in the US bought the printer's manuscript of this book for $35 million (£25.3 million) in September 2017.

Bestselling comics

Micky Maus (Germany), *The Beano* and *Classics Illustrated* (both English language)

Each of these comics (picture books) are thought to have sold 1 billion copies.

Bestselling fiction book

Don Quixote

First published in 1605 in Spain, Miguel de Cervantes's story of the nobleman Don Quixote and his companion, Sancho Panza, has sold an estimated 500 million copies.

> More **books** are published in **China** per year than in any other country —440,000 in 2013.

First woman to fly solo from Britain to Australia
In May 1930, Englishwoman Amy Johnson took off in her Gipsy Moth plane from an airstrip in Croydon, England. She flew 11,000 miles (17,700 km) to land in Darwin, Australia, 19 days later. The first person to fly solo from Britain to Australia was Australian Bert Hinkler in 1928.

Earhart was the first woman to fly across the Atlantic Ocean in 1928—as a passenger.

First woman to fly solo across the Atlantic Ocean
Another brave flyer, American Amelia Earhart flew across the Atlantic Ocean in May 1932. The trip from Canada to Northern Ireland took her 15 hours. Charles Lindberg was the first person to complete the flight solo in his plane *Spirit of St Louis* in 1927.

First deep dive
Americans William Beebe and Otis Barton ventured deep underwater inside a submersible called a bathysphere in 1934. They descended to a depth of 3,000 ft (900 m).

Adventurers

These brave individuals **pushed the limits** of experience by **venturing farther** than anyone had gone before. Some **set off alone**; others traveled **higher or deeper** into the unknown.

TANZANIA
BATHYSCAPHE TRIESTE 1960

First to reach the deepest part of the ocean

Jacques Piccard from Switzerland and American Don Walsh were the first to reach the bottom of the Mariana Trench, a place called Challenger Deep, which is the very deepest part of the ocean. In 1960, they traveled in a bathyscaphe named *Trieste*, to a depth of 35,814 ft (10,916 m).

First person to sail solo around the world

Englishman Francis Chichester set sail from Plymouth, England, in August 1966. After 107 days, he reached Sydney, Australia, then he returned via Cape Horn, taking 119 days and covering 29,630 miles (47,685 km) in total.

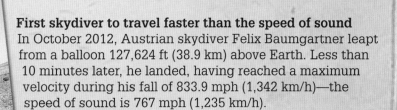

First skydiver to travel faster than the speed of sound

In October 2012, Austrian skydiver Felix Baumgartner leapt from a balloon 127,624 ft (38.9 km) above Earth. Less than 10 minutes later, he landed, having reached a maximum velocity during his fall of 833.9 mph (1,342 km/h)—the speed of sound is 767 mph (1,235 km/h).

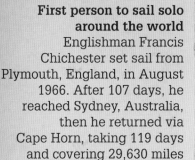

These adventurers planned their journeys for months or years before they set off. Often the vehicles or vessels they traveled in had to be tested and adapted for the trip first.

FAST FACTS

The record set by Felix Baumgartner was beaten in 2014 by former Google executive Alan Eustace, who leapt from 135,826 ft (41.4 km)—7,874 ft (2.4 km) higher than Baumgartner. Both jumped from the stratosphere, which starts at 9 miles (14.5 km) above Earth. Jumbo jets fly at 39,000 ft (11.8 km).

Alan Eustace
135,826 ft (41.4 km)

Felix Baumgartner
127,624 ft (38.9 km)

Jumbo Jet
39,000 ft (11.8 km)

High achievers

Scaling **Everest**, the **highest mountain** on Earth, must surely be the **peak** of these adventurers' achievements.

1975
The first **female** to the top was Junko Tabei (Japan), while Lhakpa Sherpa (Nepal) has summited seven times.

1953
Sir Edmund Hillary (New Zealand) and **Tenzing Norgay** (Nepal) are officially the first people ever to reach the summit.

2001
First to descend on a snowboard Marco Siffredi (France) achieved the feat in 2001 but died while trying to repeat the descent the following year.

2001
The only blind **explorer** to the peak was Erik Weihenmayer (US), who has also conquered all of the Seven Summits.

Although the first successful ascent of Mount Everest occurred more than 60 years ago, there are many more records to be had, from the first woman to the youngest person; and then there are the descents, too.

1933

First to fly over the peak were Royal Air Force pilots Lord Clydesdale (Douglas Douglas-Hamilton) and David McIntyre, in a two-seater biplane.

SPEEDY SUMMIT

In 2017, Spanish climber Kilian Jornet ascended Everest twice in one week without ropes or oxygen. He set the fastest time from Advance Base Camp (at 21,000 ft/6,400 m) to the summit: 17 hours. It normally takes four days.

1993

Aged 19, India's Dicky Dolma was the first female teenager to climb Everest. The youngest climber to date is 13-year-old American Jordan Romero.

2013

Aged 80, Yuichiro Miura of Japan is the oldest man to summit. He is 7 years older than Tamae Watanabe, the oldest woman to the top.

Yuichiro Miura, the oldest person to summit, broke the record at age **70,** then at **75,** and again at **80!**

1922

First attempts, led by Charles G. Bruce and Edward Lisle Strutt (both from England), didn't reach the summit but set a world record for the highest climb: 27,320 ft (8,326 m).

THE ROOF OF THE WORLD

Since 1921, 10 major expeditions had failed in the quest to climb Mount Everest, the world's highest mountain. But on May 29, 1953, 33-year-old Edmund Hillary (New Zealand) and 38-year-old Tenzing Norgay (Nepal) achieved everlasting fame when they became the first to stand on top of the 29,029-ft (8,848-m) peak.

Under the sea

The depths of the **oceans** are tough to explore, though some men and women have **pushed the limits** and dived deeper than anyone else.

Years of training and peak physical fitness are needed to break diving records. The men and women on these pages used these qualities to achieve astonishing underwater feats. Whether using minimal equipment or special sleds and suits, the most important thing is to have a very cool head.

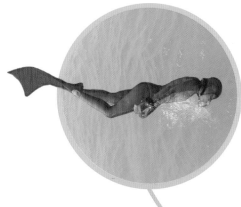

Deepest female freedive
331 ft (101 m)
Russian Natalia Molchanova became the first woman to dive deeper than 328 ft (100 m) in 2009 when she reached 331 ft (101 m) in Sharm el Sheikh, Egypt. The dive lasted 3 minutes 50 seconds.

Deepest male freedive
400 ft (122 m)
William Trubridge from New Zealand broke the world record for freediving in 2016, when he reached a depth of 400 ft (122 m). Trubridge held his breath for 4 minutes 24 seconds while making the dive.

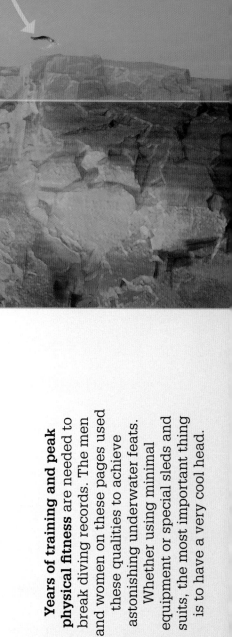

328 ft
100 m

SCUBA

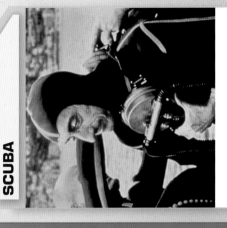

Frenchmen Jacques Cousteau and Émile Gagnon invented the first open-circuit, self-contained underwater breathing apparatus (SCUBA) in 1942–43. It allowed divers to spend more time underwater.

Deepest SCUBA dive
1,090 ft (332.5 m)
In 2014, in the Red Sea, Ahmed Gabr, an Egyptian, set a new record for a diver using SCUBA equipment.

Orcas dive to depths of 866 ft (264 m) while they are hunting.

656 ft 200 m

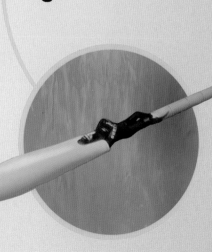

Deepest "no-limits" freedive
702 ft (214 m)
Herbert Nitsch, an Austrian freediver, reached a world-record-breaking depth of 702 ft (214 m) in Greece in 2007. In a type of freediving called "no limits," he used a weighted sled to descend and an air-filled balloon to come back to the surface.

984 ft 300 m

1,312 ft 400 m

1,640 ft 500 m

Deepest dive in a diving suit
2,000 ft (609.6 m)
A US Navy diver, Daniel P. Jackson, set a new record for diving in an atmospheric diving suit (ADS) in California in 2006. The suit was designed to withstand the extreme pressure at 2,000 ft (609.6 m) underwater.

1,968 ft 600 m

First to discover Northwest Passage
In 1906, Norwegian explorer Roald Amundsen (far left) became the first to journey through this important trade route across the Arctic, which connects the Atlantic and Pacific Oceans.

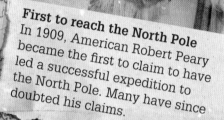

First to reach the North Pole
In 1909, American Robert Peary became the first to claim to have led a successful expedition to the North Pole. Many have since doubted his claims.

First undisputed flight over the North Pole
The brainchild of Roald Amundsen and Italian airship designer Umberto Nobile, the airship *Norge* made the first verified flight of any kind over the North Pole on May 12, 1926.

First surface traveler known to have reached the North Pole
On April 20, 1968, American Ralph Plaisted, using a snowmobile, completed a 43-day journey to the North Pole. His trip was the first verified overland journey to the pole.

The **USS Nautilus**'s trip under the polar ice cap was known as **Operation Sunshine**.

Arctic records

The **Arctic region** is one of the world's most **inhospitable** environments and has proved one of the most **challenging** and **difficult** places on Earth for explorers.

First watercraft to reach the North Pole
On August 3, 1958, the USS *Nautilus*, the world's first nuclear-powered submarine, became the first watercraft to reach the geographic North Pole. It went on to travel underneath the entire polar ice cap.

The North Pole is the world's most northerly point. When you are standing there, any direction you point is south. No one actually lives at the North Pole, but expeditions to reach it started in the 19th century.

FAST FACTS

There is no land at the North Pole. Instead, it is covered by floating ice, known as pack ice, which is between 9 and 13 ft (3 and 4 m) thick. Depending on the time of year, this pack ice covers an area of between 3.47 and 4.63 million sq miles (9 and 12 million sq km).

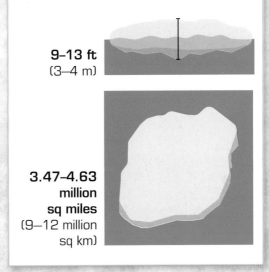

9–13 ft
(3–4 m)

3.47–4.63 million sq miles
(9–12 million sq km)

Fastest trek to the North Pole
In 1995, Russian Misha Malakhov (above, right) and Canadian Richard Weber took 123 days to trudge to the North Pole and back, dragging everything they needed behind them on 300-lb (136-kg) sleds.

Antarctic records

Antarctica was the **last** of Earth's seven continents to be **discovered**. At the turn of the 20th century, the quest to become the first to reach the **South Pole** became the **greatest prize** in exploration.

First to reach the South Pole
Norwegian Roald Amundsen led a party of five to become the first to reach the South Pole. They arrived there on December 14, 1911, beating a British team, led by Robert F. Scott, by 34 days.

First permanent base in Antarctica
Ormond House—a meteorological (weather) observatory on Laurie Island (the second largest of the South Orkney Islands)—was established by the Scottish National Antarctic Expedition in 1903.

AMUNDSEN vs. SCOTT

Amundsen		Scott
5 men		**17** men
3 tons of supplies		**1 ton** of supplies
52 huskies		**0** huskies

Amundsen's mission to the South Pole was planned to perfection. An experienced polar explorer, he took exactly what was required. The graphic above shows the stark difference between the equipment taken by Amundsen and that taken by Scott.

First to sight Antarctica
On January 28, 1820, the crew of the Russian ship Vostok, captained by Admiral Fabian Gottlieb von Bellingshausen (above), became the first to sight Antarctica's coastline.

H POLAR CHAR
100

First flight over the South Pole
On November 28, 1929, American Richard Byrd (above) along with pilot Bernt Balchen, copilot Harold June, and photographer Ashley McKinley, became the first person to fly over the South Pole.

First overland crossing of Antarctica
On March 2, 1958, members of the Commonwealth Trans-Antarctic Expedition, led by Englishman Vivien Fuchs (right) and Edmund Hillary (NZ, left), completed the first successful overland crossing of Antarctica. They covered 2,158 miles (3,473 km).

Emilio Marcos Palma (Argentina) was the first to be born on mainland Antarctica, in 1978.

Antarctica has the highest average elevation of any continent in the world—7,545 ft (2,300 m). The South Pole itself sits on top of the Antarctic Plateau at a height of 9,301 ft (2,835 m).

First all-women's team to reach the South Pole
On January 14, 1993, four women of the American Women's Expedition (led by Ann Bancroft, above) became the first all-women's team to reach the South Pole. It took them 67 days to achieve the feat.

I'm a survivor

Pushed to the **limits**, these people have all proved their **strength** and **stamina** by **staying alive** in some of the most **extreme conditions** and **environments** on Earth.

Longest time ADRIFT AT SEA

When a storm in October 1813 damaged Captain Oguri Jukichi's ship off the coast of Japan, he and two crewmates were adrift for 484 days. Only in March 1815 did another ship come to the rescue. Luckily, some of the ship's cargo was soybeans, which kept them alive.

Lowest body TEMPERATURE

In 1999 Norwegian radiologist Anna Bågenholm survived the lowest body temperature ever recorded when she fell under ice while skiing. Her temperature dropped to 56.7°F (13.7°C)— a healthy body temperature is 98.6°F (37°C).

FAST FACTS

The "rule of three" says people can survive for...

3 minutes without air

3 hours without shelter (unless in icy water)

3 days without water (if sheltered from harsh environment)

3 weeks without food (if you have water and shelter)

This is just a guide: a person may last three hours without shelter in freezing conditions, but not if they are wet, which makes hypothermia set in more quickly. In icy water, survival time is just three minutes.

Longest time TRAPPED UNDERGROUND

When the San José copper-gold mine in Chile collapsed in 2010, it left 33 miners underground. They remained trapped for a record-breaking 69 days until a rescue mission lifted them 2,257 ft (688 m) to safety.

Most time on a DESERT ISLAND

From 1704 to 1709, Alexander Selkirk spent four years and four months castaway on an island off the coast of Chile. The British naval officer's experience inspired the famous novel *Robinson Crusoe* (1719) by Daniel Defoe.

Longest time in the DESERT

American Robert Bogucki wandered in the Great Sandy Desert, Australia, on a spiritual quest for 43 days before being rescued in 1999. He was located by the crew of a TV company helicopter, which had been following the second search team.

Not everyone on this page is an accidental hero. While Captain Jukichi and the Chilean miners were simply going about their (admittedly dangerous) jobs when disaster struck, Alexander Selkirk chose to live on a desert island.

Sporting prowess

When it comes to sports, only the best and the most dedicated make it to the very top of their game. Records are set and broken as champions blow away the competition to add their names to the sporting world's honor roll.

Brazil's captain, Cafu, holds aloft the soccer World Cup trophy after his team's 2–0 victory over Germany in the 2002 final. Following tournament victories in 1958, 1962, 1970, and 1994, it was the country's fifth success in the competition—the most by any country in the tournament's history.

FIRST CHAMPION

American James Connolly is credited as being the first modern Olympic champion. He won the opening event at the 1896 Games held in Athens—the long jump.

Most medals (male)
American swimmer Michael Phelps is the runaway winner with 28 Olympic medals, including 23 golds. He won eight golds in Beijing, 2008—the most golds in a single Games.

Most medals (female)
Soviet (Russian) gymnast Larisa Latynina won a record-breaking 18 Olympic medals between 1956 and 1964.

Larisa Latynina's record for **most medals** stood for **48 years** before Michael Phelps broke it.

Michael Phelps

Larisa Latynina

Olympic achievers

All athletes **go for gold** at the **Olympics**, aiming to fulfill the motto of "**Faster, Higher, Stronger**." But who is the **best of the best**?

Trischa Zorn

Most successful Paralympian
American swimmer Trischa Zorn, who was born blind, won 55 medals during her career—41 of them gold—between 1980 and 2004.

Sir Steve Redgrave

The original Olympics of ancient Greece did not award medals, but wreaths made of olive branches. The winners at the first modern Olympics in 1896 didn't receive gold medals either. Instead they received silver ones and olive wreaths. Gold medals were finally introduced in 1904.

Usain Bolt

Endurance medals
British rower Sir Steve Redgrave is the only athlete to win golds for an endurance event at five different Olympics, from 1984 to 2000.

Fastest sprinter
Speedy eight-time gold-medal runner Usain Bolt was the first person to complete the double-triple of winning the 100 m, 200 m, and 4 x 100 m relay at consecutive Olympics (2012 and 2016).

FAST FACTS

Summer medals

	2,522	1,010	849		
US					
		Soviet Union			
			Great Britain		

Winter medals

368	305	238
Norway	US	Germany

The US has won the most Olympic medals up to 2016. They're the leaders for Summer Games medals but are second behind Norway for the most Winter Games wins.

OTHER GOAL-SCORING RECORDS

Most goals scored at the World Cup: 16—Miroslav Klose (Germany, 2002–2014).

Most goals scored at a single World Cup: 13—Just Fontaine (France, 1958).

Most goals scored in a single World Cup match: 5—Oleg Salenko (Russia) vs. Cameroon, 1994.

Most goals scored in a World Cup final: 3—Geoff Hurst (England) vs. West Germany, 1966.

Most goals scored in a career: 1,468—Josef Bican (Austria), in 918 matches between 1931 and 1956.

Most international goals: 109—Ali Daei (in 149 matches for Iran between 1993 and 2006).

Most goals scored in a single international match: 13—Archie Thompson (Australia) vs. American Samoa. Australia won the qualifying match for the 2002 World Cup 31–0.

Most goals in a calendar year: 91—Lionel Messi (for Barcelona and Argentina in 2012).

Begovic's goal was not enough to win the match, however. It ended in a 1–1 draw.

Just 13 seconds into Stoke City's Premier League match against Southampton on November 2, 2013, Stoke goalkeeper Asmir Begovic kicked a back pass upfield. The ball soared through the air, bounced just outside the Southampton penalty area, flew over the opposing keeper's head, and nestled in the back of the net. The length of the shot: 301.5 ft (91.9 m).

GOAL!!!

Soccer is the **world's most popular sport**. Many thousands of matches have been played in every corner of the globe, but what is the **longest goal ever scored** in an official match?

The record-breaking shot was helped by a strong following wind.

The record for the most **goals** scored by **a goalkeeper is 131, by** Rogério Ceni (Brazil).

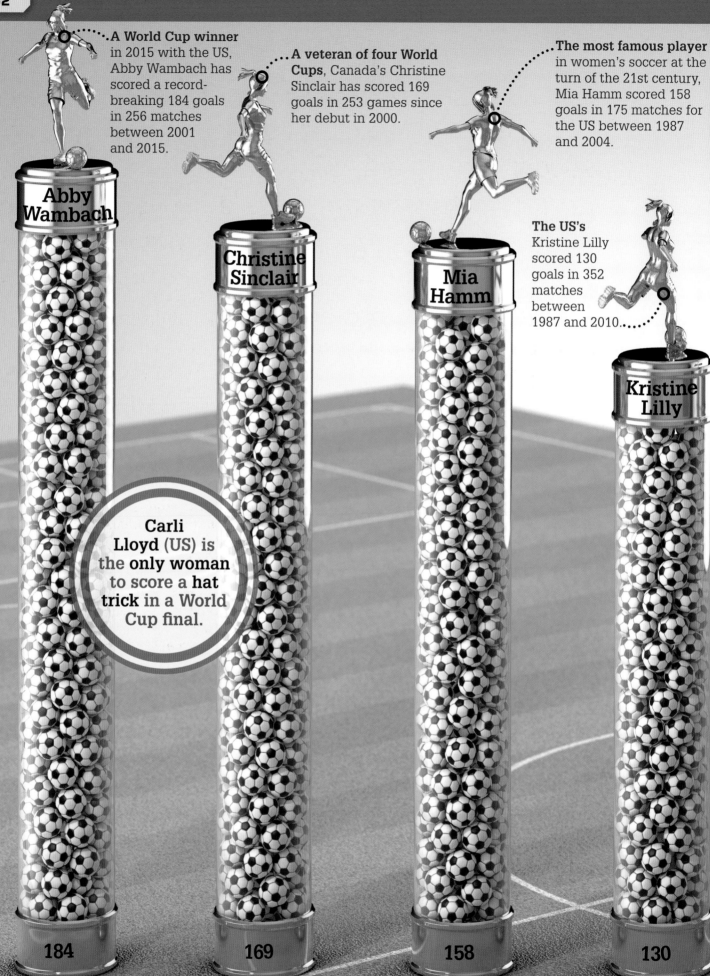

A World Cup winner in 2015 with the US, Abby Wambach has scored a record-breaking 184 goals in 256 matches between 2001 and 2015.

A veteran of four World Cups, Canada's Christine Sinclair has scored 169 goals in 253 games since her debut in 2000.

The most famous player in women's soccer at the turn of the 21st century, Mia Hamm scored 158 goals in 175 matches for the US between 1987 and 2004.

The US's Kristine Lilly scored 130 goals in 352 matches between 1987 and 2010.

Abby Wambach

Christine Sinclair

Mia Hamm

Kristine Lilly

Carli Lloyd (US) is **the only woman to score a hat trick** in a World Cup final.

184

169

158

130

Hot shots

The **first** official women's international soccer match was played in **1971**—99 years after the first men's match. But that has not stopped **women soccer players** from producing some **record-breaking** performances.

Germany's two-time World Cup winner Birgit Prinz scored 128 goals in 214 matches between 1994 and 2011.

Fifteen women have scored more than 100 goals in women's international soccer. Here are the top five.

Birgit Prinz

128

WOMEN'S WORLD CUP GOAL-SCORING RECORDS

Leading goal scorer: Marta (Brazil, below)—15 goals in four tournament appearances between 2003 and 2015.

Most goals scored in a single tournament: 10—Michelle Akers (US) in 1991.

Most goals in a single match: 5—Michelle Akers (US) vs. Chinese Taipei on November 24, 1991.

Fastest hat trick: 5 minutes—Fabienne Humm (Switzerland) against Ecuador on June 12, 2015.

Fastest goal from kickoff: 30 seconds—Lena Videkull (Sweden) against Japan on November 19, 1991.

Youngest goal scorer: Elena Danilova (Russia) was 16 years 107 days old when she scored against Germany on October 2, 2003.

Oldest goal scorer: Formiga (Brazil) was 37 years 98 days old when she scored against South Korea on June 9, 2015.

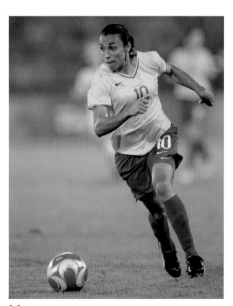

Marta

Home-run heroics

Baseball is a sport that is particularly associated with **numbers**, but perhaps the best-known number of all is **73**: the record for the highest number of **home runs** hit in a **single season**

PERFECT PITCHING

Most complete games in an MLB career: 749—Cy Young (between 1890 and 1911). A complete game is when a pitcher throws an entire game without a relief pitcher.

Most no-hitters in a career: 7—Nolan Ryan (between 1966 and 1993). A no-hitter is a game in which a team was not able to get a single player onto first base.

Most career shutouts: 110—Walter Johnson (between 1907 and 1927). A shutout is when a pitcher pitches a complete game and does not allow the opposing team to score a run.

Most career strikeouts: 5,714—Nolan Ryan (between 1966 and 1993). A strikeout is when a batter records three strikes at a single at bat.

Cal Ripken Jr. played a record **2,632 consecutive games** between 1982 and 1999.

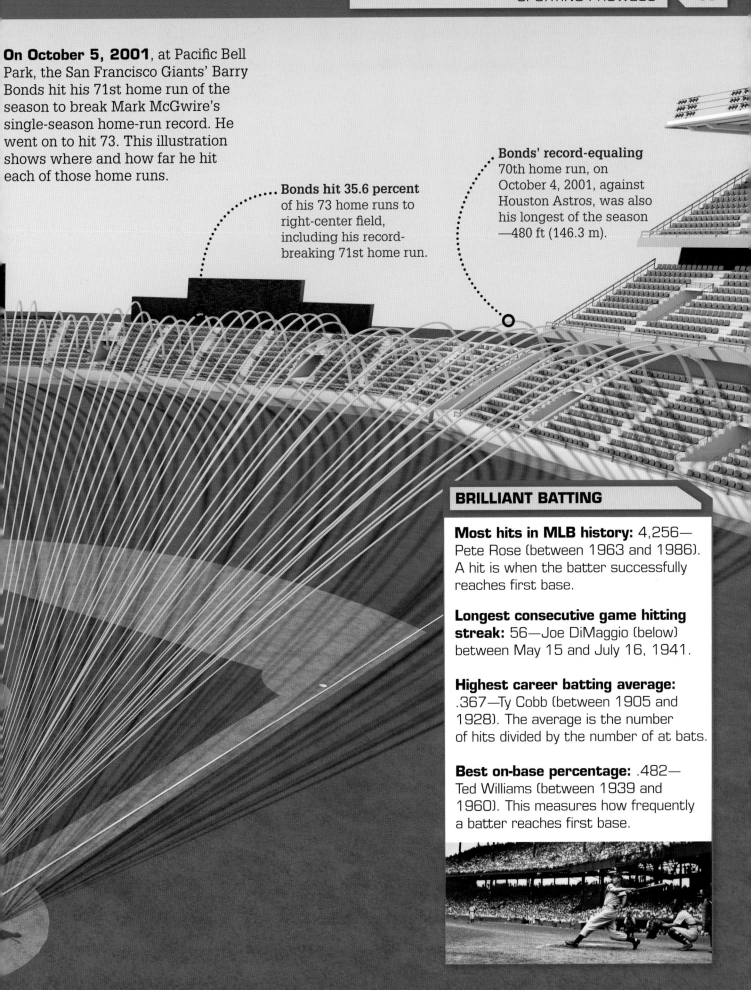

On October 5, 2001, at Pacific Bell Park, the San Francisco Giants' Barry Bonds hit his 71st home run of the season to break Mark McGwire's single-season home-run record. He went on to hit 73. This illustration shows where and how far he hit each of those home runs.

Bonds hit 35.6 percent of his 73 home runs to right-center field, including his record-breaking 71st home run.

Bonds' record-equaling 70th home run, on October 4, 2001, against Houston Astros, was also his longest of the season —480 ft (146.3 m).

BRILLIANT BATTING

Most hits in MLB history: 4,256— Pete Rose (between 1963 and 1986). A hit is when the batter successfully reaches first base.

Longest consecutive game hitting streak: 56—Joe DiMaggio (below) between May 15 and July 16, 1941.

Highest career batting average: .367—Ty Cobb (between 1905 and 1928). The average is the number of hits divided by the number of at bats.

Best on-base percentage: .482— Ted Williams (between 1939 and 1960). This measures how frequently a batter reaches first base.

Motorsport is hugely **popular** in all corners of the world, but of the sport's big four categories—Formula One, IndyCar, NASCAR, and MotoGP—which has produced the fastest vehicle?

Formula One

- Most championships: 7—Michael Schumacher (Germany, above)
- Most race wins: 91—Michael Schumacher (Germany)
- Most pole positions: 72—Lewis Hamilton (GB)
- Most constructors' championships: 16—Ferrari

IndyCar

- Most championships: 7—A.J. Foyt (US, above)
- Most race wins: 67—A.J. Foyt (US)
- Most pole positions: 65—Mario Andretti (US)
- Most constructors' wins: 198—Team Penske (most race wins)

MotoGP

- Most championships: 8—Giacomo Agostini (Italy)
- Most race wins: 89—Valentino Rossi (Italy, above)
- Most pole positions: 73—Marc Márquez (Spain)
- Most constructors' championships: 23—Honda

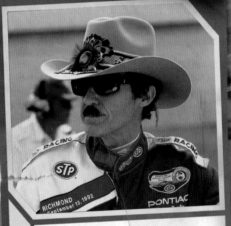

NASCAR

- Most championships: 7—Richard Petty (above), Dale Earnhardt Jr., Jimmie Johnson
- Most race wins: 200—Richard Petty
- Most pole positions: 123—Richard Petty
- Most constructors' championships: 38—Chevrolet

231.486 mph (372.54 km/h)
Formula One
Valtteri Bottas (Finland) hit this jaw-dropping speed at the 2016 Mexican Grand Prix.

Kings of the road

People have **raced** on two wheels and on four for as long as **motorcycles and cars** have been around, but who have proved the true **masters of motorsport**?

NASCAR's **Richard Petty** celebrated a world record **200 race wins** during his career.

212.809 mph (342.483 km/h)
NASCAR
Bill Elliott (US) recorded NASCAR's fastest-ever speed at Talladega, Alabama, on April 30, 1987.

220.4 mph (354.7 km/h)
MotoGP
Michele Pirro (Italy) became MotoGP's king of speed at the 2017 Italian Grand Prix.

237.498 mph (382.216 km/h)
IndyCar
Arie Luyendyk (Netherlands) clocked this speed in qualifying for the 1996 Indy 500 in Indiana.

Sport data

FANTASTIC SOCCER RECORDS

MOST WORLD CUP WINS

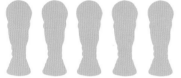

5 **BRAZIL** (1958, 1962, 1970, 1994, 2002)

4 **GERMANY** (1954, 1974, 1990, 2014)
ITALY (1934, 1938, 1982, 2006)

2 **ARGENTINA** (1978, 1986)
URUGUAY (1930, 1950)

1 **ENGLAND** (1966)
FRANCE (1998)
SPAIN (2010)

MOST WOMEN'S WORLD CUP WINS

3 **US** (1991, 1999, 2015)

2 **GERMANY** (2003, 2007)

1 **NORWAY** (1995)
JAPAN (2011)

MOST SUCCESSFUL SOCCER TEAMS

MOST SUCCESSFUL TEAMS AT THE EUROPEAN CHAMPIONSHIPS: Germany (1972, 1980, 1996) and Spain (1964, 2008, 2012) have both won the title on three occasions.

MOST SUCCESSFUL TEAM AT THE COPA AMERICA: Uruguay has claimed the title on 15 occasions, one more than Argentina.

MOST SUCCESSFUL TEAM IN THE CHAMPIONS LEAGUE: Real Madrid (Spain) has won the tournament on 12 occasions, including five straight wins between 1956 and 1960. Milan (Italy) lies second on the list with seven victories.

MOST SUCCESSFUL TEAM IN THE COPA LIBERTADORES: Independiente (Argentina) is the tournament's most successful team, with seven victories. Compatriots Boca Juniors are second on the list with six wins.

MOST SUCCESSFUL DOMESTIC TEAM IN HISTORY: Rangers (Scotland) have won their domestic league a world record 54 times.

HIGHEST SCORE

The **highest score** in a competitive soccer match is **149–0**, in a match between **SO l'Emyrne** and **AS Adema** in Madagascar on October 31, 2002. Enraged by the performance of the officials in their previous match, SO l'Emyrne scored 149 own goals!

ICE HOCKEY GREAT

Wayne Gretzky —dubbed **the Great One**—is the most **famous player in NHL history**. He holds **numerous all-time records.** Here are the best of them:

MOST POINTS IN A SINGLE SEASON: 215 IN 1985–1986

MOST POINTS IN A CAREER: 2,857 POINTS

MOST REGULAR SEASON POINTS PER GAME: 1.921

MOST REGULAR SEASON GOALS: 894

MOST REGULAR SEASON ASSISTS: 1,963

MOST PLAYOFF POINTS: 382

HOOP HEROICS

BASKETBALL

MOST CONSECUTIVE WINS IN AN NBA SEASON: 33—LA Lakers in the 1971–1972 season (the second-best mark in NBA history is 22 consecutive wins).

NBA SINGLE-GAME SCORING RECORD: 100 points—Wilt Chamberlain, for the Philadelphia Warriors versus the New York Knicks on March 2, 1962. *The closest anyone has gotten to the record since is 81 points—Kobe Bryant, for the LA Lakers against the Toronto Raptors on January 22, 2006.*

MOST CONSECUTIVE NBA TITLES: 8—Boston Celtics between 1959 and 1966.

MOST ASSISTS IN AN NBA CAREER: 15,806—John Stockton *(the closest active player is Jason Kidd, who is 3,500 assists behind Stockton's mark).*

MOST CAREER NBA POINTS: 33,387—Kareem Abdul-Jabbar, between 1969 and 1989.

MOST CONSECUTIVE NBA GAMES WITH 10 POINTS OR MORE: 866—Michael Jordan, between 1986 and 2001.

GRIDIRON GREATS

FOOTBALL

BIGGEST VICTORY: Georgia Tech beat Cumberland University by the staggering margin of 220–0 in a college match on October 7, 1916.

MOST CONSECUTIVE NFL GAMES PLAYED: 297—Brett Favre. He played in every consecutive match for 19 seasons between 1992 and 2010, playing for three teams—Green Bay Packers, New York Jets, and Minnesota Vikings.

THE LONGEST PLAY IN NHL HISTORY: 109.88 yards—Antonio Cromartie playing for the San Diego Chargers against the Minnesota Vikings on April 11, 2007. He returned a missed field goal for a touchdown.

MOST CAREER RECEIVING YARDS: 122,985 yards—Jerry Rice (between 1985 and 2004). His record-breaking total is 6,961 yards ahead of the next best on the list (Terrell Owens).

MOST CAREER RECEPTIONS: 1,549—Jerry Rice.

MOST CAREER RUSHING YARDS: 18,355—Emmitt Smith.

MOST CONSECUTIVE GAMES WITH A TOUCHDOWN PASS: 47—Johnny Unitas (set between 1956 and 1960 while playing for the Baltimore Cubs).

MOST PASSING TOUCHDOWNS (CAREER): 539—Peyton Manning (between 1998 and 2015).

MOST SUPER BOWL WINS: 6—Pittsburgh Steelers (1974, 1975, 1978, 1979, 2005, 2008).

Top-class long jumpers reach a **speed of 33 ft/s (10 m/s)** on the runway.

Athletes try to reach the ideal speed before takeoff.

GIANT LEAP

It may no longer be the world record, but Bob Beamon's jump at the 1968 Olympics is the most famous long jump in history. The American's leap of 29.2 ft (8.90 m) broke the existing world record by 17.7 in (45 cm).

The current long jump world record was set by US athlete Mike Powell at the 1991 World Championships in Tokyo, Japan—29.36 ft (8.95 m). That's the equivalent of jumping farther than the length of two original-style Volkswagen Beetles parked bumper to bumper.

Longest jump

Once in the air, the athlete will move his arms and legs forward and will try to hang in the air. This is known as the "hitch kick."

The **long jump** is a track-and-field event that requires speed, technique, and strength to **leap as far as possible** from a fixed point. It has been contested at **every Olympics** since 1896.

Mike Powell's record has now stood for more than 25 years—it is the fourth-longest-standing world record in athletics.

On landing, the athlete will try to propel his body beyond the initial landing point to increase the distance of his jump.

HISTORIC JUMPS

5 **24.7 ft (7.52 m)**—Galina Chistyakova (Russia, 1988)
The only woman in history to jump more than 24.6 ft (7.5 m).

4 **24.96 ft (7.61 m)**—Peter O'Connor (Ireland, 1901)
First record ratified by International Association of Athletics Federation.

3 **26.67 ft (8.13 m)**—Jesse Owens (US, 1935)
First jump in history to exceed 26.24 ft (8 m).

2 **29.2 ft (8.90 m)**—Bob Beamon (US, 1968)
Beamon's leap shattered the world record by 17.7 in (45 cm).

1 **29.36 ft (8.95 m)**—Mike Powell (US, 1991)
Powell beat Bob Beamon's world record leap by 2 in (5 cm).

These are the current men's and women's world records.

1 MEN'S—20.2 ft (6.16 m)
Renaud Lavillenie (2014)

2 WOMEN'S—16.6 ft (5.06 m)
Yelena Isinbayeva (2009)

The vaulter prepares for the "fly away," the easiest part of the jump. He will push off the top of the pole and rotate his body in an attempt to clear the bar.

Known as the "swing up," the vaulter swings his legs up and starts to move his arms toward his hips.

The faster the vaulter can run down the runway, and the better he can execute the takeoff, the more the pole will bend. This will help the vaulter achieve a greater height.

RENAUD LAVILLENIE

On February 15, 2014, France's 2012 Olympic champion Renaud Lavillenie broke Sergey Bubka's 21-year-old world pole vault record. He cleared an astonishing height of 20.2 ft (6.16 m) in Donetsk, Ukraine.

US vaulters won **every** pole vault **gold medal** at the Olympics between 1896 and 1968.

Athletes run up and plant the pole in a hole in the ground called a "box." Flexible poles, made of carbon fiber or fiberglass, were introduced in the 1950s, making it easier for vaulters to clear greater heights.

The current men's world record—20.2 ft (6.16 m)—is greater than the height of an average giraffe (19.7 ft/6 m).

Raising the bar

The pole vault is a **track-and-field event** in athletics in which vaulters use a **long, flexible pole to help them spring over a bar**.

The pole vault has been a full-medal event at the Olympic Games since 1896 for men and since 2000 for women. Vaulters have three attempts to clear a height or a combination of heights. If they fail to do so, they are eliminated from the competition.

After an attempt to clear the bar, the vaulter starts a long descent to the ground. A crash mat softens the impact of the landing.

YELENA ISINBAYEVA

Russia's Yelena Isinbayeva is the current women's world record holder in the pole vault. A two-time Olympic gold medalist (in 2004 and 2008), she achieved her history-making leap of 16.6 ft (5.06 m) in Zurich, Switzerland, on August 28, 2009.

The 100-m world record is the ultimate prize for a sprinter. This illustration shows some of history's most memorable 100-m runs. It compares where the athletes would have been on the track when the current men's and women's world record holders crossed the finishing line.

11.4 seconds
On October 4, 1952, Australian Marjorie Jackson became the first woman to run the 100 m in under 11.5 seconds.

11.01 seconds
West German Annegret Richter ran 11.01 seconds in the 100-m final at the 1976 Olympics in Canada.

11.04 seconds
West German Inge Helten broke the world record on June 13, 1976, and held it for 42 days.

11.07 seconds
Wyomia Tyus (US) broke the world record in the women's 100-m final at the 1968 Olympics in Mexico.

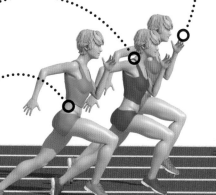

91 m   92 m   93 m   94 m   95 m

100-meter marvels

The world's **speediest sprinters** enter the 100-meter race. Winners are crowned the **fastest people on Earth**.

Usain Bolt is the only athlete to win three successive Olympic 100-m titles.

10.3 seconds
On August 3, 1930, Percy Williams (Canada) became the first athlete to run the 100 m in 10.3 seconds.

10.2 seconds
Jesse Owens (US) ran 10.2 seconds on June 20, 1936. The time would not be bettered for 20 years.

10.1 seconds
Willie Williams (US) clocked 10.1 seconds on August 3, 1956.

91 m   92 m   93 m   94 m   95 m

10.88 seconds
On July 1, 1977, East German Marlies Oelsner produced the first electronically timed sub-11-second run.

10.81 seconds
Oelsner broke her own world record on June 8, 1983, but it lasted for only 25 days.

10.79 seconds
Evelyn Ashford (US) broke Oelsner's record on July 3, 1983, and became the first woman to run under 10.8 seconds.

10.76 seconds
Ashford bettered her own world record in Zurich, Switzerland, on August 22, 1984.

10.49 seconds
Florence Griffith-Joyner (US) smashed Ashford's world record by 0.3 seconds on July 16, 1988.

96 m   97 m   98 m   99 m   100 m

FASTEST WOMAN

American Florence Griffith-Joyner (Flo-Jo) has the fastest female feet in history, holding both the 100-m and 200-m world records. In 1988, Flo-Jo set a new 100-m record of 10.49 seconds.

FASTEST MAN

Jamaican Usain Bolt is the fastest man ever in the 100 m and 200 m. Nicknamed "Lightning Bolt," he made history by running the 100 m in 9.58 seconds at the World Championships in Berlin in 2009.

9.95 seconds
Jim Hines (US) ran the first sub-10-second 100 m at the 1968 Olympics.

9.93 seconds
Calvin Smith (US) finally broke Jim Hines's record on July 3, 1983.

9.86 seconds
Carl Lewis (US) twice equalled Smith's record and finally broke it on August 25, 1991.

9.79 seconds
On June 16, 1999, Maurice Greene (US) became the first to break the 9.8 barrier.

9.69 seconds
Usain Bolt (Jamaica) smashed Greene's world record at the 2008 Olympics in Beijing, China.

9.58 seconds
Usain Bolt set the current world record mark at the 2009 World Championships in Berlin, Germany.

96 m   97 m   98 m   99 m   100 m

LIGHTNING BOLT

Usain Bolt is the fastest man on the planet.
The Jamaican has run the three fastest-ever times
in the 100 m and is the current 200 m world
record holder. He is also the only man in history
to win the 100 m—200 m double at three
consecutive Olympics (in 2008, 2012, and 2016).

Amazing athletes

THESE ARE THE CURRENT **WORLD RECORD HOLDERS** FOR THE MAJOR ATHLETIC EVENTS:

MEN'S FIELD EVENTS

EVENT	RECORD	ATHLETE (COUNTRY)	LOCATION	DATE
HIGH JUMP	2.45 M	JAVIER SOTOMAYOR (CUBA)	SALAMANCA, SPAIN	JULY 27, 1993
POLE VAULT	6.16 M	RENAUD LAVILLENIE (FRANCE)	DONETSK, UKRAINE	FEBRUARY 15, 2014
LONG JUMP	8.95 M	MIKE POWELL (US)	TOKYO, JAPAN	AUGUST 30, 1991
TRIPLE JUMP	18.29 M	JONATHAN EDWARDS (GB)	GOTHENBURG, SWEDEN	AUGUST 7, 1995
SHOT PUT	23.12 M	RANDY BARNES (US)	WESTWOOD, CA, US	MAY 20, 1990
DISCUS THROW	74.08 M	JÜRGEN SCHULT (EAST GERMANY)	NEUBRANDENBURG, EAST GERMANY	JUNE 6, 1986
HAMMER THROW	86.74 M	YURIY SEDYKH (RUSSIA)	STUTTGART, GERMANY	AUGUST 30, 1986
JAVELIN THROW	98.48 M	JAN ZELEZNY (CZECH REPUBLIC)	JENA, GERMANY	MAY 25, 1996
DECATHLON	9,045 PTS	ASHTON EATON (US)	BEIJING, CHINA	AUGUST 29, 2015

WOMEN'S FIELD EVENTS

EVENT	RECORD	ATHLETE (COUNTRY)	LOCATION	DATE
HIGH JUMP	2.09 M	STEFKA KOSTADINOVA (BULGARIA)	ROME, ITALY	AUGUST 30, 1987
POLE VAULT	5.06 M	YELENA ISINBAYEVA (RUSSIA)	ZURICH, SWITZERLAND	AUGUST 28, 2009
LONG JUMP	7.62 M	GALINA CHISTYAKOVA (USSR)	LENINGRAD, USSR	JUNE 11, 1988
TRIPLE JUMP	15.50 M	INESSA KRAVETS (UKRAINE)	GOTHENBURG, SWEDEN	AUGUST 10, 1995
SHOT PUT	22.63 M	NATALYA LISOVSKAYA (USSR)	MOSCOW, RUSSIA	JUNE 7, 1987
DISCUS THROW	76.80 M	GABRIELE REINSCH (EAST GERMANY)	NEUBRANDENBURG, EAST GERMANY	JULY 9, 1988
HAMMER THROW	82.98 M	ANITA WLODARCZYK (POLAND)	WARSAW, POLAND	AUGUST 28, 2016
JAVELIN THROW	72.28 M	BARBORA SPOTAKOVA (CZECH REPUBLIC)	STUTTGART, GERMANY	SEPTEMBER 13, 2008
HEPTATHLON	7,291 PTS	JACKIE JOYNER-KERSEE (US)	SEOUL, SOUTH KOREA	SEPTEMBER 24, 1988

MEN'S TRACK EVENTS

EVENT	RECORD	ATHLETE (COUNTRY)	LOCATION	DATE
100 M	9.58s	USAIN BOLT (JAMAICA)	BERLIN, GERMANY	AUGUST 16, 2009
200 M	19.19s	USAIN BOLT (JAMAICA)	BERLIN, GERMANY	AUGUST 20, 2009
400 M	43.03s	WAYDE VAN NIEKERK (SOUTH AFRICA)	RIO DE JANEIRO, BRAZIL	AUGUST 14, 2016
800 M	1:40.91	DAVID RUSHIDA (KENYA)	LONDON, ENGLAND	AUGUST 9, 2012
1,500 M	3:26.00	HICHAM EL GUERROUJ (MOROCCO)	ROME, ITALY	JULY 14, 1998
5,000 M	12:37.35	KENENISA BEKELE (ETHIOPIA)	HENGELO, NETHERLANDS	MAY 31, 2004
10,000 M	26:17.53	KENENISA BEKELE (ETHIOPIA)	BRUSSELS, BELGIUM	AUGUST 26, 2005
MARATHON	2:02:57	DENNIS KIPRUTO KIMETTO (KENYA)	BERLIN, GERMANY	SEPTEMBER 29, 2014
100 M HURDLES	12.80s	ARIES MERRITT (US)	BRUSSELS, BELGIUM	SEPTEMBER 7, 2012
400 M HURDLES	46.78s	KEVIN YOUNG (US)	BARCELONA, SPAIN	AUGUST 6, 1992
4 X 100 RELAY	36.84s	JAMAICA	LONDON, ENGLAND	AUGUST 11, 2012
4 X 400 RELAY	1:18.63	US	STUTTGART, GERMANY	AUGUST 22, 1993

WOMEN'S TRACK EVENTS

EVENT	RECORD	ATHLETE (COUNTRY)	LOCATION	DATE
100 M	10.49s	FLORENCE GRIFFITH-JOYNER (US)	INDIANAPOLIS, IN, US	JULY 16, 1988
200 M	21.34s	FLORENCE GRIFFITH-JOYNER (US)	SEOUL, SOUTH KOREA	SEPTEMBER 29, 1988
400 M	47.60s	MARITA KOCH (EAST GERMANY)	CANBERRA, AUSTRALIA	OCTOBER 6, 1985
800 M	1:53.28	JARMILA KRATOCHVILOVA (CZECHOSLOVAKIA)	MUNICH, GERMANY	JULY 26, 1983
1,500 M	3:50.07	GENZEBE DIBABA (ETHIOPIA)	FONTVIEILLE, SWITZERLAND	JULY 17, 2015
5,000 M	14:11.15	TIRUNESH DIBABA (ETHIOPIA)	OSLO, NORWAY	JUNE 6, 2008
10,000 M	29:17.45	ALMAZ AYANA (ETHIOPIA)	RIO DE JANEIRO, BRAZIL	AUGUST 12, 2016
MARATHON	2:15.25	PAULA RADCLIFFE (GB)	LONDON, ENGLAND	APRIL 13, 2003
100 M HURDLES	12.20s	KENDRA HARRISON (US)	LONDON, ENGLAND	JULY 22, 2016
400 M HURDLES	52.34s	YULIYA PECHONKINA (RUSSIA)	TULA, RUSSIA	AUGUST 8, 2003
4 X 100 RELAY	40.82s	US	LONDON, ENGLAND	AUGUST 10, 2012
4 X 400 RELAY	3:15.17	USSR	MOSCOW, RUSSIA	AUGUST 4, 1984

A rule passed after 1976 required an Olympian to be at least 16 years old. This means Comaneci's record for being the youngest-ever all-around gymnastics champion will never be beaten.

IMPERFECT SCOREBOARD

The organizers of the 1976 Olympics did not believe anyone could score a perfect 10, so they made room for only three digits on the scoreboard. When Comaneci's score was revealed to the crowd, it showed only 1.00.

SWISS TIMING

073

1.00

Comaneci is the Olympics' youngest-ever all-around gymnastics champion.

Having already been awarded the Olympic Games' first-ever perfect 10 for her routine on the parallel bars, 14-year-old Nadia Comaneci went on to receive six more 10s, including one for this perfomance on the balance beam

Perfect 10

In 1976, **Romanian gymnast Nadia Comaneci** became the first person to achieve a **perfect 10** at an Olympics gymnastics event. But this was only the first of **seven standout performances** at the 1976 Games in Montreal, Canada, which made **sporting history**.

Comaneci's balance beam was flawless as she dazzled the crowd with graceful and fluid movements and unmatched steadiness......

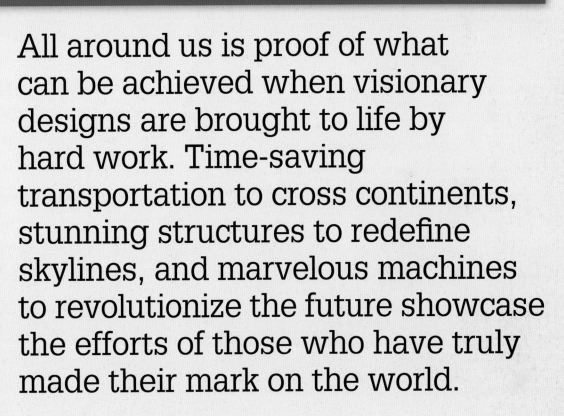

Feats of engineering

All around us is proof of what can be achieved when visionary designs are brought to life by hard work. Time-saving transportation to cross continents, stunning structures to redefine skylines, and marvelous machines to revolutionize the future showcase the efforts of those who have truly made their mark on the world.

Dubai's skyscrapers poke through the early-morning clouds. The emirate is famous for its super-high structures and is home to the world's tallest building (the Burj Khalifa at 2,717 ft/828 m), the tallest hotel (the JW Marriott Marquis at 1,165 ft/355 m), and the tallest residential building (the Princess Tower at 1,355 ft/413 m).

On the road

Start your **engines**, it's time to take a **trip** down memory **lane** to discover which **inventors** came **first** in the ultimate **road race**.

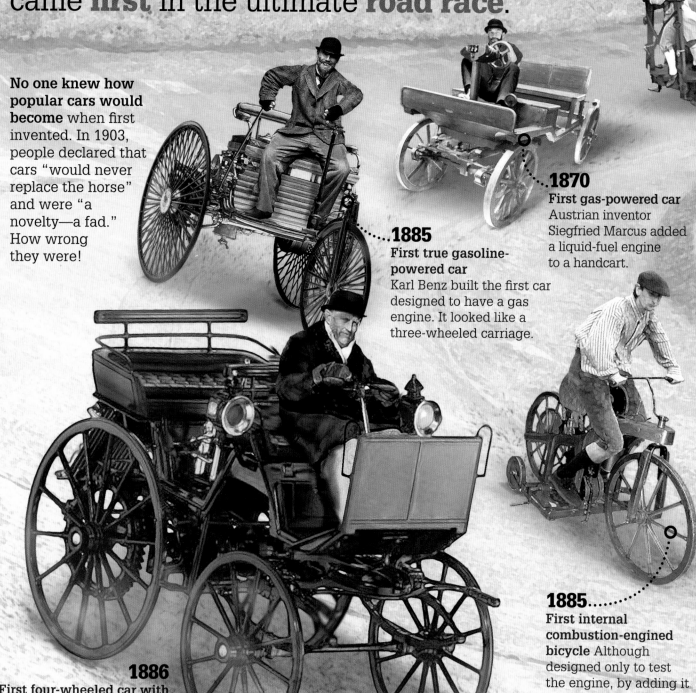

No one knew how popular cars would become when first invented. In 1903, people declared that cars "would never replace the horse" and were "a novelty—a fad." How wrong they were!

1870
First gas-powered car
Austrian inventor Siegfried Marcus added a liquid-fuel engine to a handcart.

1885
First true gasoline-powered car
Karl Benz built the first car designed to have a gas engine. It looked like a three-wheeled carriage.

1885
First internal combustion-engined bicycle Although designed only to test the engine, by adding it to a bike, Gottlieb Daimler invented the first true motorcycle.

1886
First four-wheeled car with a four-stroke engine
This was built by German engineers Gottlieb Daimler and Wilhelm Maybach.

TOPPING 100

A car named *La Jamais Contente* was the first car to top 62 mph (100 km/h), in 1899. Driver Camille Jenatzy achieved 65.79 mph (105.88 km/h) over a distance of 0.6 miles (1 km) in his Belgian-made electric car.

1769
First full-scale car
Frenchman Nicolas-Joseph Cugnot invented a steam-powered tricycle that he called the "steam dray," meaning a cart powered by steam.

1801
First passenger-carrying car
On its test run, Richard Trevithick's *Puffing Devil* carried eight people uphill at a speed of 4 mph (6.4 km/h).

1894
First mass-produced motorcycle
The Hildebrand & Wolfmüller factory in Germany was the first to make motorbikes in large numbers; they produced more than 1,000 in two years.

1888
First true electric car
The *Flocken Elektrowagen*, invented by Andreas Flocken, is said to be the first practical electric car.

Full steam ahead

Steam trains were once a **common sight** on the world's railways. The trains shown here were all the **fastest** trains **of their time**.

Stephenson's *Rocket* reached a speed of 30 mph (48 km/h) in 1830.

Many of the *Rocket*'s innovations were so successful that they set the basic layout for locomotives right until the end of the steam era.

On November 30, 1934, the *Flying Scotsman* became the first train to travel at more than 100 mph (161 km/h).

The *Mallard* reached a top speed of 126 mph (202.6 km/h) on July 3, 1938.

Stephenson's fabled *Rocket*, built for the Liverpool and Manchester Railway in 1829, was the template for steam trains for the next 150 years. The *Flying Scotsman* and the *Mallard* were perhaps the most iconic steam trains of their time.

MALLARD

THE FLYING SCOTSMAN

The *Flying Scotsman* hauled the nonstop London to Edinburgh service.

BIG BOY

Known as "Big Boy," the American Locomotive Company 4000-class steam locomotive had the longest engine body of any locomotive ever built—85.3 ft/25.99 m.

Air pioneers

Imagine being the **first** pilot. Flying **unknown routes** with **untested technology**, these **aviators** must have been **incredibly brave**.

The first **transatlantic flight** took 16 hours. The same journey today takes 5 hours.

1970

The first Boeing 747, or jumbo jet, flew between New York and London. The first wide-body plane, it held the record for most passengers (500) until the arrival of the Airbus in 2007.

Wright Flyer

1903

The first controlled, powered flight took place in the US with Orville and Wilbur Wright's *Wright Flyer*. It was only in the air for 12 seconds, but the age of flight had begun.

Bell X-1

 FAST FACTS

It's not just planes that have set pioneering flight records.

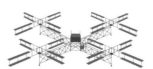

1783 First manned, untethered flight: the Montgolfier brothers' hot-air balloon took passengers over Paris, France.

1804 First flight by heavier-than-air machine: George Cayley built and flew the first working glider.

1907 First manned helicopter flight: the Breguet brothers' Gyroplane No.1 lifted 2 ft (0.6 m) into the air.

The sky was not the limit for these intrepid travelers. Each of them has set a record in aviation, whether for being the first aircraft of its type, flying a longer distance, or increasing speed to supersonic.

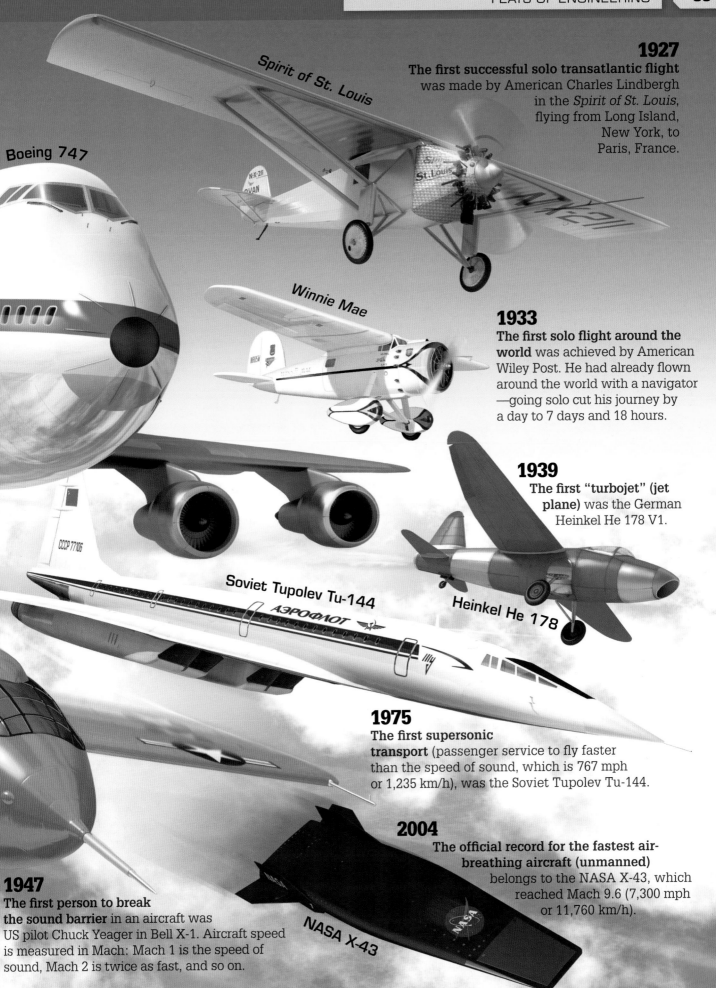

Spirit of St. Louis

Boeing 747

1927
The first successful solo transatlantic flight was made by American Charles Lindbergh in the *Spirit of St. Louis*, flying from Long Island, New York, to Paris, France.

Winnie Mae

1933
The first solo flight around the world was achieved by American Wiley Post. He had already flown around the world with a navigator —going solo cut his journey by a day to 7 days and 18 hours.

1939
The first "turbojet" (jet plane) was the German Heinkel He 178 V1.

Soviet Tupolev Tu-144

Heinkel He 178

1975
The first supersonic transport (passenger service to fly faster than the speed of sound, which is 767 mph or 1,235 km/h), was the Soviet Tupolev Tu-144.

2004
The official record for the fastest air-breathing aircraft (unmanned) belongs to the NASA X-43, which reached Mach 9.6 (7,300 mph or 11,760 km/h).

1947
The first person to break the sound barrier in an aircraft was US pilot Chuck Yeager in Bell X-1. Aircraft speed is measured in Mach: Mach 1 is the speed of sound, Mach 2 is twice as fast, and so on.

NASA X-43

The need for speed

The world's official **land-speed record** is a staggering **763.035 mph** (1,227.985 km/h). It was set by British RAF fighter pilot **Andy Green** on October 15, 1997, in a vehicle called **Thrust SSC**.

FUTURE CHALLENGER

Plans are underway to attempt to break the land-speed record. The British-designed *Bloodhound* is planned to travel at more than 1,000 mph (1,609 km/h).

Two Rolls-Royce Spey 205 turbojet engines powered the vehicle. These engines are normally found on British F-4 Phantom II jet fighters.

📊 FAST FACTS

There are several speed-based records up for grabs.

317.58 mph (511.09 km/h)

Water-speed record by Ken Warby in *Spirit of Australia*, 1978

376.363 mph (605.697 km/h)

Motorcycle record by Rocky Robinson in *Top Oil-Ack Attack*, 2010

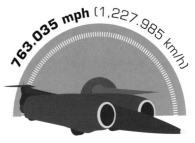

763.035 mph (1,227.985 km/h)

Land-speed record by Andy Green in Thrust SSC, 1997

Although the car was designed and built in Britain, the world-record attempt took place in the Black Rock Desert, Nevada. The desert's flat, lake-bed surface made it the perfect site for land-speed record attempts. To set the record, Andy Green had to drive *Thrust* twice within an hour, in opposite directions over a measured distance of 1 mile (1.6 km).

The SSC was the **first car** to travel **faster than the speed of sound.**

The engines burned 4 gallons (18 liters) of fuel per second.

763.035 mph (1,227.985 kph)

Including the streamlined tail fin, the car's total length was 54 ft (16.5 m). It was 12 ft (3.7 m) wide and weighed 10.5 tons (10.7 tonnes).

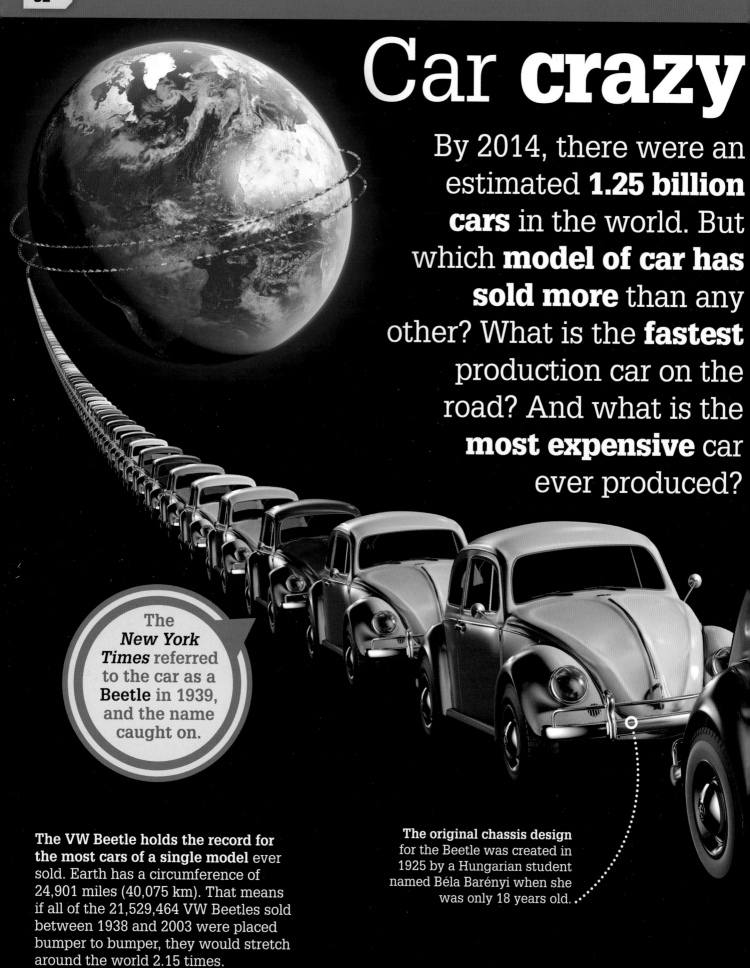

Car **crazy**

By 2014, there were an estimated **1.25 billion cars** in the world. But which **model of car has sold more** than any other? What is the **fastest** production car on the road? And what is the **most expensive** car ever produced?

The *New York Times* referred to the car as a **Beetle** in 1939, and the name caught on.

The VW Beetle holds the record for the most cars of a single model ever sold. Earth has a circumference of 24,901 miles (40,075 km). That means if all of the 21,529,464 VW Beetles sold between 1938 and 2003 were placed bumper to bumper, they would stretch around the world 2.15 times.

The original chassis design for the Beetle was created in 1925 by a Hungarian student named Béla Barényi when she was only 18 years old.

OTHER RECORD-BREAKING CARS

The world's bestselling car: Toyota Corolla—40 million of these cars have been sold since the name was first launched in 1966 (although there have been many different models).

The world's smallest car: The UK-made Peel P50 was 54 in (137.2 cm) long, 39 in (99.1 cm) wide, and weighed 130 lb (59 kg). Only 50 of them were ever made.

Quickest to 62 mph (100 km/h): The 2015 Porsche 918 Spyder is the world's fastest-accelerating car. It can go from 0–62 mph (0–100 km/h) in just 2.2 seconds.

The fastest production car ever built: The Swedish-made Koenigsegg Agera RS has a top speed of 277.9 mph (447.2 km/h)—the fastest of any production car ever built.

Most powerful engine in a production car: The Bugatti Chiron is the world's most powerful car, producing 1,479 brake horsepower. It has a top speed of 261 mph (420 km/h).

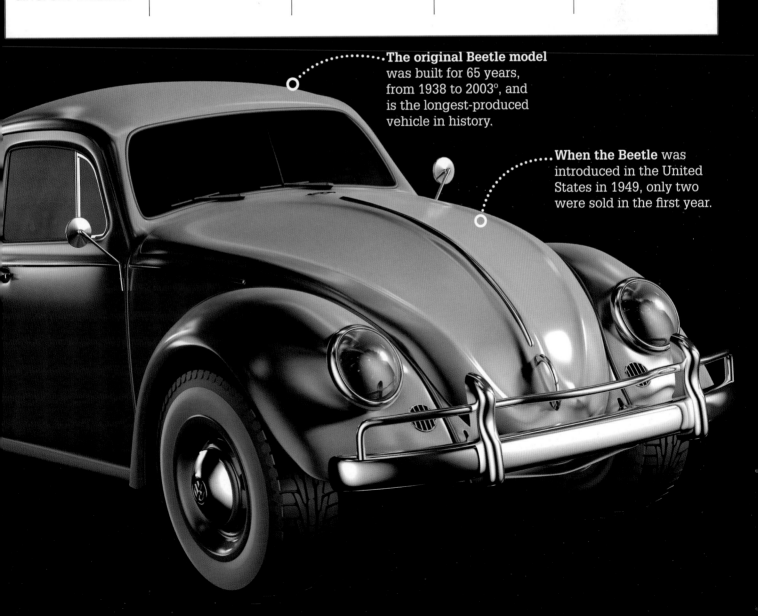

The original Beetle model was built for 65 years, from 1938 to 2003°, and is the longest-produced vehicle in history.

When the Beetle was introduced in the United States in 1949, only two were sold in the first year.

On the right track

TRAILBLAZING TRAINS

The fastest train on a national railway system:
A TGV V150 (above) reached a world record speed of 357.16 mph (574.8 km/h) on the high-speed line between Paris and Strasbourg in France on April 3, 2007.

The fastest train:
A Central Japan Railway Company maglev train ran at a speed of 374.68 mph (603 km/h) on a test track on April 21, 2005.

The longest train route:
The world's longest train route runs 6,346 miles (10,214 km) between Moscow (Russia) and Pyongyang (North Korea). It takes 206 hours to complete the journey.

The route, one of the world's most picturesque, passes towering peaks, shimmering lakes, and gigantic glaciers.

The train carriages are pressurized, like the cabin on a plane. Oxygen levels are increased as the train reaches higher altitudes.

Technology has **transformed** the way people travel. **Trains** today enable us to go **higher, faster, and farther** than ever before.

The Qinghai–Tibet railway is 1,215 miles (1,956 km) long and connects the cities of Xining (China) and Lhasa (Tibet). The line includes the world's highest section of railway 16,640 ft (5,072 m).

The **journey** from Xining to Lhasa takes **20 hours and 55 minutes** to complete.

The trains were specially designed to work at the extreme altitude. Around 597 miles (960 km) of the track sit above 13,123 ft (4,000 m).

This ship has **16 decks** and a **waterslide** with a **100-ft (30.5-m) drop.**

Biggest cruise ship
Launched in 2018, *Symphony of the Seas* is 1,188 ft (362 m) long and 215 ft (65 m) wide, with room for 5,500 passengers in 2,774 cabins.

Longest limo
American Dream was the longest car ever made. The 100-ft (30.5-m) customized limousine featured 24 wheels and a central hinge for turning corners. A heliport and Jacuzzi enhanced this luxurious limo!

From colossal cruise ships to sumptuous superyachts and lavish limousines, here are some of the biggest and most expensive forms of transportation ever built.

Most expensive car
One of only 39 ever made, a 1962 Ferrari 250 GTO Berlinetta was sold in 2014 for $38,115,000 (£27,345,000), making it the most expensive car ever sold at auction.

Travel in style

All aboard! Whether traveling by land or sea, these **record-breaking** cars, boats, and ships are **first class** all the way.

SYMPHONY OF THE SEAS

Biggest superyacht
Built in 2013 in Germany, *Azzam* measures 592 ft (180 m). The water-jet propulsion system allows it to reach a speed of 31.5 knots— 36 mph (58 km/h).

Most expensive yacht
History Supreme is worth an estimated $4.8 billion (£3.4 billion). This is because 220,000 lb (100,000 kg) of gold and platinum coats its hull, dining area, deck, rails, and anchor.

Awesome aircraft

Largest airship:
Hindenburg LZ 129
804 ft (245 m) long

Creating bigger and better aircraft has been a challenge since the first powered flight in 1903. But size isn't always an indication of superiority: the Hindenburg (which carried a maximum of 72 passengers) lasted just 14 months before being destroyed by fire in 1937.

Largest cargo aircraft:
Antonov An-225
276 ft (84 m) long

Largest commercial passenger aircraft:
Airbus A380
240 ft (73 m) long

Largest flying boat:
Hughes H-4 Hercules
219 ft (67 m) long

From **huge wingspans** to the ability to carry **great weights** or just being the **largest** of their type, here are some of the **biggest** aircraft to have flown.

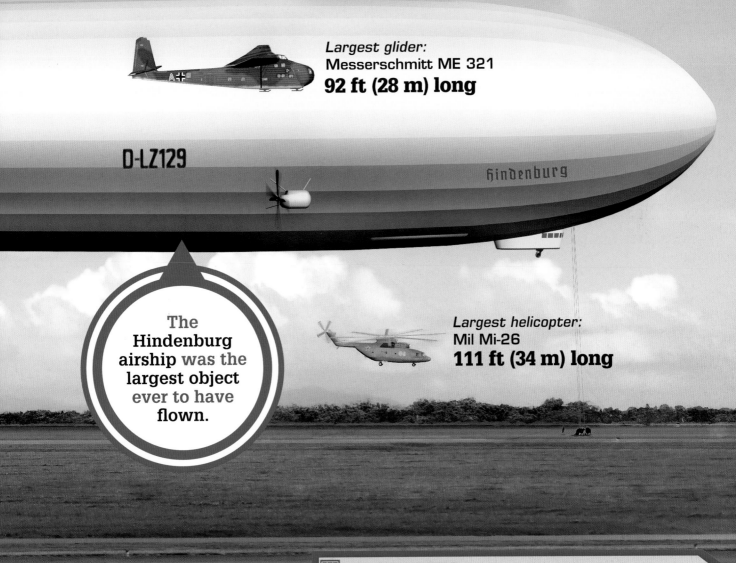

Largest glider:
Messerschmitt ME 321
92 ft (28 m) long

D-LZ129

Hindenburg

The Hindenburg airship was the largest object ever to have flown.

Largest helicopter:
Mil Mi-26
111 ft (34 m) long

Largest biplane:
Navy Curtiss NC-4
68 ft (20.8 m) long

📊 FAST FACTS

The smallest plane that could carry a person was the Bumble Bee II, a biplane that made one flight in 1988 before crashing. It was smaller than an Airbus A380 engine and had a wingspan just 5.5 ft (1.68 m) wide.

A380 engine fan:
9.7 ft (2.95 m) wide

Bumble Bee II:
8.8 ft (2.69 m) long

GIANT OF THE SKY

At 804 ft (245 m) in length, the *Hindenburg* was the largest rigid airship ever built and still holds the record as the largest aircraft ever to fly. It was built in Germany and flew from March 1936 until it was destroyed by fire on May 6, 1937, while attempting to land at Lakehurst, New Jersey.

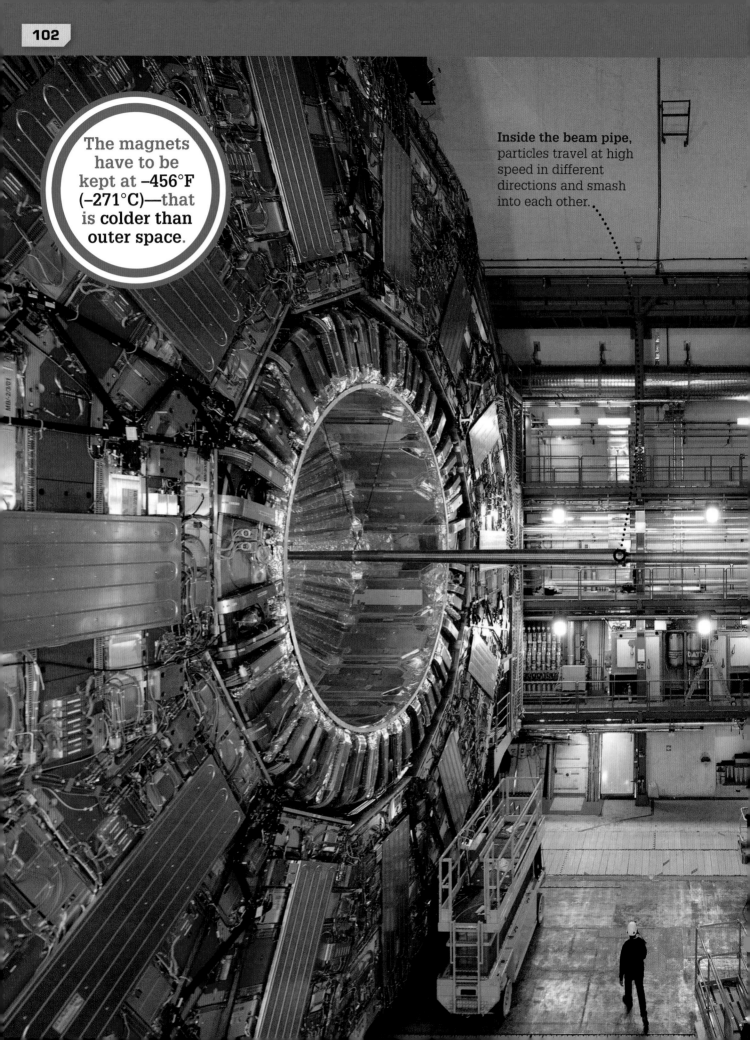

The magnets have to be kept at –456°F (–271°C)—that is colder than outer space.

Inside the beam pipe, particles travel at high speed in different directions and smash into each other.

Colossal collider

Deep underground in France and Switzerland lies the **Large Hadron Collider**—the world's **largest machine** and **most powerful** particle accelerator. Scientists are using it to find out more about **particle physics**.

The Large Hadron Collider is conducting an experiment on a huge scale. It is smashing together two beams of particles at super-high speed around its vast 17-mile-long (27-km-long) ring. Scientists are trying to reproduce what happened during the Big Bang.

UNDERGROUND EXPERIMENTS

The particle accelerator is made up of two circular tunnels underground. The yellow and blue lines drawn on this photograph show the route of the tunnels. Inside them, the particles are made to travel at close to the speed of light and collide at four locations. Each area is conducting a different experiment into forces and energy.

Mega machines

Some machines are **mind-bogglingly big**. They can be used to **shift earth**, to **carry enormous objects** (such as space rockets), or to help **dig open-pit mines**.

Giant buckets on this huge wheel carve through the earth.

At 315 ft (96 m) tall, Bagger 293 is also the world's highest terrestrial vehicle.

LARGEST SELF-POWERED VEHICLE

Weighing 6 million lb (2,721 tonnes) and measuring 131 x 114 ft (40 x 35 m), NASA's Crawler Transporter (used to carry spacecraft) is the world's largest self-powered vehicle.

Weighing a colossal 31.3 million lb (14,200 tonnes), the Bagger 293 Bucket Excavator is the world's heaviest land vehicle. It belongs to a German mining company and is used to excavate an enormous mine near Hambach, western Germany.

RWE 288

KRUPP
SIEMENS

Bagger 293 removes enough material to fill **2,500 railroad cars** every day.

Wonder walls

Walls have been built for **thousands of years** to give **privacy**, **defense**, **protection**, and even **segregation**. Those that have stood the **test of time** still make history today.

In 1985, three Chinese friends became the first to walk the wall; it took them 508 days.

Longest Roman wall
Hadrian's Wall extends for 73 miles (117 km) across the north of England. It holds records for the world's longest Roman wall, the oldest Roman artifact, and the longest wall in Europe. The Roman emperor Hadrian ordered that it be built in 122 CE to provide protection from the Barbarians in the north.

World's longest wall
The Great Wall of China, stretching a whopping 5,500 miles (8,851 km) across the north of China, is the world's longest wall. It was first built to protect China against invaders from the north. Some sections of the wall are 39 ft (12 m) tall and 32 ft (10 m) thick.

Oldest temple walls
The oldest temple walls ever discovered support the glorious temple of Gobekli Tepe in Sanliurfa, Turkey. These great carved stones were carefully positioned by ancient builders about 11,500 years ago.

Oldest city walls
The first city walls were built around the ancient city of Jericho, Israel. Built from about 8000 BCE, these strong stone walls stand 13 ft (4 m) high.

Longest walls around a fort
The longest walls around a fort or castle are found at Kumbhalgarh Fort in Rajasthan, India. Built in the 15th century, the walls measure 22 miles (36 km) long and 16 ft (5 m) wide. Legends claim eight horses could run along side by side on top of the walls!

Walls have been built for centuries around castles and cities or along national borders to keep people in or out. The world's oldest walls have become historic and iconic landmarks.

📈 FAST FACTS

The Great Wall of China is one of the most popular places in the world to visit. Here are a few more tourist attractions and the number of visitors per year.

Las Vegas Strip, US	Grand Bazaar, Turkey	Great Wall of China, China	Eiffel Tower, France
39 million visitors	15 million visitors	9 million visitors	7 million visitors

Breathtaking bridges

Today's bridges are far more than just a means of crossing a river or another impassable object; some are **astonishing feats of engineering** that have to be seen to be believed.

The Duge Bridge, near Liupanshui, China, is the highest bridge in the world. Its road deck sits 1,854 ft (565 m) above the Beipan River at the bottom of the steep valley below.

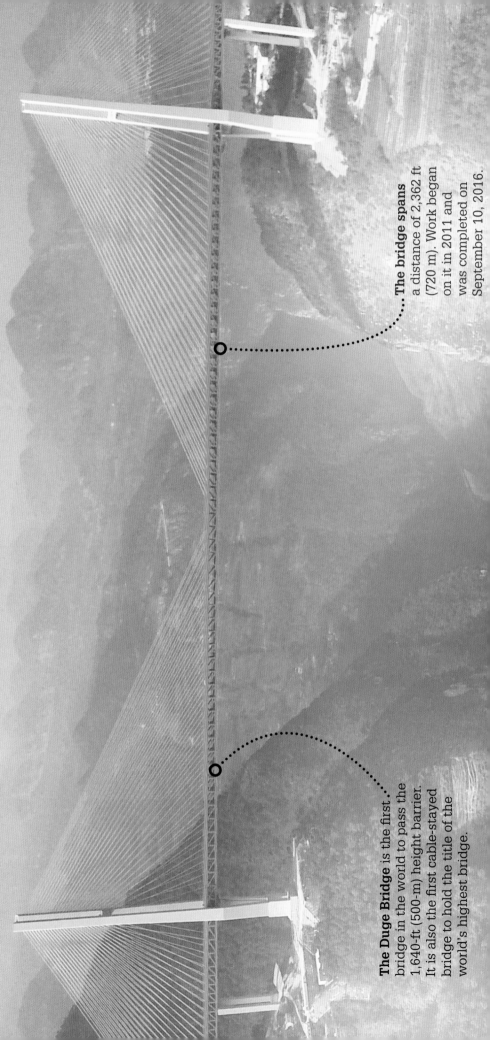

The bridge spans a distance of 2,362 ft (720 m). Work began on it in 2011 and was completed on September 10, 2016.

The Duge Bridge is the first bridge in the world to pass the 1,640-ft (500-m) height barrier. It is also the first cable-stayed bridge to hold the title of the world's highest bridge.

The **bridge** would tower over Kuala Lumpur's Petronas (Twin) Towers, which, at 1,480 ft (451.9 m), were the world's tallest buildings between 1998 and 2004.

The world's oldest, usable bridge crosses the Meles River, Turkey. It dates to **850** BCE.

TALLEST AND LONGEST

World's tallest bridge: The Millau Viaduct, France (below), is 1,125 ft (343 m) from the top of the structure to the bottom.

World's longest bridge: The Danyang-Kunshan Grand Bridge, on the Shanghai–Beijing railway in China is a staggering 102.4 miles (164.8 km) long.

Longest bridge over water (continuous): Lake Pontchartrain Causeway in Louisiana is 23.89 miles (38.442 km) long.

Longest cable-stayed bridge: Russky Bridge, in Vladivostok, Russia, has a span of 3,622 ft (1,104 m).

Hitting record-breaking heights

Throughout history, a total of **25 structures** have held the accolade of being the **world's tallest building**. The title currently belongs to the 2,717-ft (828-m) **Burj Khalifa** in Dubai, UAE.

THE GREATEST OF THE PYRAMIDS

The Great Pyramid of Giza, situated near Cairo, Egypt, was built over a period of 20 years, ending around 2560 BCE. At 481 ft (146.6 m), it was the tallest man-made structure in the world for a record-breaking 3,800 years.

The earliest of the world's tallest buildings were pyramids and religious structures. However, the increased use of steel in construction from the late 19th century eventually led to the birth of the skyscraper.

**Chrysler Building,
New York, US**
1,046 ft (318.8 m)
1930–1931

**Woolworth Building,
New York, US**
792 ft (241.4 m)
1913–1930

**Great Pyramid of Giza,
near Cairo, Egypt**
481 ft (146.6 m)
2560 BCE–1240 CE

**Old St. Paul's
Cathedral,
London, UK**
493 ft (150.2 m)
1240–1311

**Lincoln Cathedral,
UK**
525 ft (160 m)
1311–1549

**St. Mary's Church,
Stralsund, Germany**
495 ft (151 m)
1549–1647

**Strasbourg
Cathedral, France**
466 ft (142 m)
1647–1847

FAST FACTS

The Jeddah Tower
in Saudi Arabia is set to become the world's tallest building on completion, which is due in 2020. At a staggering 3,281 ft (1,000 m) tall, it will be 564 ft (172 m) taller than the current record holder, Dubai's Burj Khalifa.

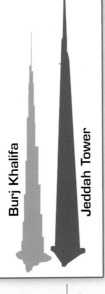

Burj Khalifa

Jeddah Tower

It is **10°F (6°C) cooler** at the **top** of the Burj Khalifa than it is at the **bottom**.

Taipei 101,
Taipei, Taiwan
1,671 ft (509.2 m)
2004–2010

Sears Tower,
Chicago, US
1,450 ft (442 m)
1974–1998

Empire State Building,
New York, US
1,250 ft (381 m)
1931–1972

World Trade Center,
New York, US
1,368 ft (417 m)
1972–1974

Petronas Towers,
Kuala Lumpur, Malaysia
1,480 ft (451.9 m)
1998–2004

Burj Khalifa,
Dubai, UAE
2,717 ft (828 m)
2010–

Jeddah Tower,
Saudi Arabia
3,281 ft
(1,000 m)

Engineering data

MEGA BUILDINGS

Big buildings aren't always **high**; some simply **cover an enormous area**. Here are two of the **world's biggest buildings by volume.**

LARGEST FLOOR AREA
OPENED IN 2013, **THE NEW CENTURY GLOBAL CENTER IS A MULTIPURPOSE BUILDING IN CHENGDU, CHINA.** IT HAS THE LARGEST FLOOR AREA OF ANY BUILDING IN THE WORLD—**18 MILLION SQ FT (1.7 MILLION SQ M)**. IT'S SO BIG, THE PRINCIPALITY OF **MONACO COULD FIT INSIDE IT.**

WORLD'S LARGEST MUSEUM
ORIGINALLY BUILT AS A FORTRESS, **THE LOUVRE, IN PARIS, FRANCE, IS THE WORLD'S LARGEST MUSEUM.** IT COVERS AN AREA OF **2.26 MILLION SQ FT (210,000 SQ M)**.

TERRIFIC TUNNELS

TUNNELS are used to **TRANSPORT TRAINS, CARS,** and even **WATER.** Some pass **under mountains**, and others even go **under the sea**, but which are **THE WORLD'S LONGEST?**

LONGEST ROAD TUNNEL:
LAERDAL TUNNEL (LAERDAL, AURLAND, NORWAY)—15.2 MILES (24.51 KM)

LONGEST UNDERSEA TUNNEL:
CHANNEL TUNNEL (ENGLAND–FRANCE)—23.5 MILES (37.9 KM)

WORLD'S LONGEST TUNNEL WITH UNDERSEA SECTION:
SEIKAN TUNNEL (JAPAN)—36 MILES (57.85 KM), OF WHICH 14.5 MILES (23.3 KM) LIE UNDER THE SEABED.

LONGEST WATER SUPPLY TUNNEL:
DELAWARE AQUEDUCT (NEW YORK, US)—85.1 MILES (137 KM)

Carved through the **Swiss Alps**, the **Gotthard Base Tunnel**, opened on June 1, 2016, is the **longest railway tunnel** in the world.

Chrüzlistock
8,914 FT (2,717 M)

 NORTH (to Zurich, Switzerland)

SWITZERLAND

LONGEST RAILWAY TUNNEL: GOTTHARD BASE TUNNEL (SWITZERLAND)—35.5 MILES (57.1 KM)

WORK IN PROGRESS

Some buildings don't get finished: some start with huge ambitions before **being abandoned**; others are **still not completed** more than **one hundred years** after **work started on them**.

WORK ON THE SAGRADA FAMILIA, AN ORNATE CATHEDRAL DESIGNED BY THE FAMOUS ARTIST GAUDÍ IN BARCELONA, SPAIN, WAS STARTED IN 1882. IT STILL HAS NOT BEEN FINISHED TO THIS DAY.

THE NAKHEEL TOWER IN DUBAI, UAE, WAS DESIGNED TO BE THE TALLEST TOWER IN THE WORLD. AT MORE THAN 3,280 FT (1 KM) TO THE SPIRE. WORK STARTED IN 2008 BUT WAS CANCELED IN 2009 HAVING RACKED UP COSTS OF MORE THAN $38 BILLION (£27.3 BILLION).

BRILLIANT BUILDINGS

Not all buildings are made of **concrete** or **bricks**. Here are some **unusual big builds** from **around the world**.

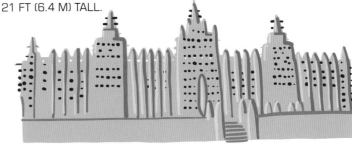

TALLEST WOODEN PAGODA

BUILT BACK IN 1056, THE SAKYAMUNI PAGODA IN SHANXI, CHINA, STANDS 220.8 FT (67.31 M) TALL. IT HAS ENDURED MORE THAN 960 YEARS OF HARSH WEATHER AND EVEN EARTHQUAKES.

BIGGEST PAPER BUILDING

THAI PAPER HOUSE WAS CONSTRUCTED IN BANGKOK, THAILAND, IN OCTOBER 2003. MADE ENTIRELY OF PAPER, IT MEASURED 49.8 FT (15.2 M) WIDE, 58.7 FT (17.9 M) LONG, AND STOOD 21 FT (6.4 M) TALL.

BIGGEST MUD BUILDING

AT 328 FT (100 M) LONG, 131 FT (40 M) WIDE, AND 52 FT (16 M) TALL, THE GRAND MOSQUE OF DJENNE IN MALI IS THE WORLD'S LARGEST BUILDING MADE OF ADOBE (MUD). BASED ON AN 11TH-CENTURY DESIGN, IT WAS BUILT IN 1907.

Piz Vatgira
9,783 FT (2,982 M)

Pizzo dell' Uomo
8,737 FT (2,663 M)

The tunnel is named for the Saint-Gotthard Massif, under which it runs.

SOUTH (to Milan, Italy)

SAINT-GOTTHARD MASSIF

Living world

The natural world offers a rich and colorful tapestry of amazing animals and plants. The age of the dinosaurs saw giant contenders for size and strength. Today, a huge variety of species live alongside each other, unknowingly winning titles for the most fabulous flora and fauna on Earth.

Millions of monarch butterflies make the longest butterfly migration, flying 3,000 miles (4,830 km) from Canada and North America to California and Mexico to spend the winter. Only butterflies born in late summer and early autumn undertake this incredible round trip, and they make it only once in their lifetime.

Animal records

Which animal has the **longest nose**, the biggest eye, or the **best eyesight?** You might be **surprised** by the answers.

Animals have some remarkable abilities. Some can hear underwater, scoop up insects with their tongue, or see to fly around in the dark. Sometimes they have developed amazing features, such as a flexible trunk or a huge pointed tusk.

Longest tusk
The narwhal's extra-long tusk is actually a specially adapted tooth. It can grow up to 8.2 ft (2.5 m) long. In relation to its body size, it is the longest tusk of all.

Most powerful bite
The bite of a saltwater crocodile is measured at 5,800 Newtons—the strongest of any land animal. The great white shark has an even stronger bite of 9,000 Newtons.

Longest tongue
The giant anteater has an extraordinarily long tongue—24 in (61 cm) in length—the longest of any land animal. It is sticky and barbed so that it can pick up its main food: insects.

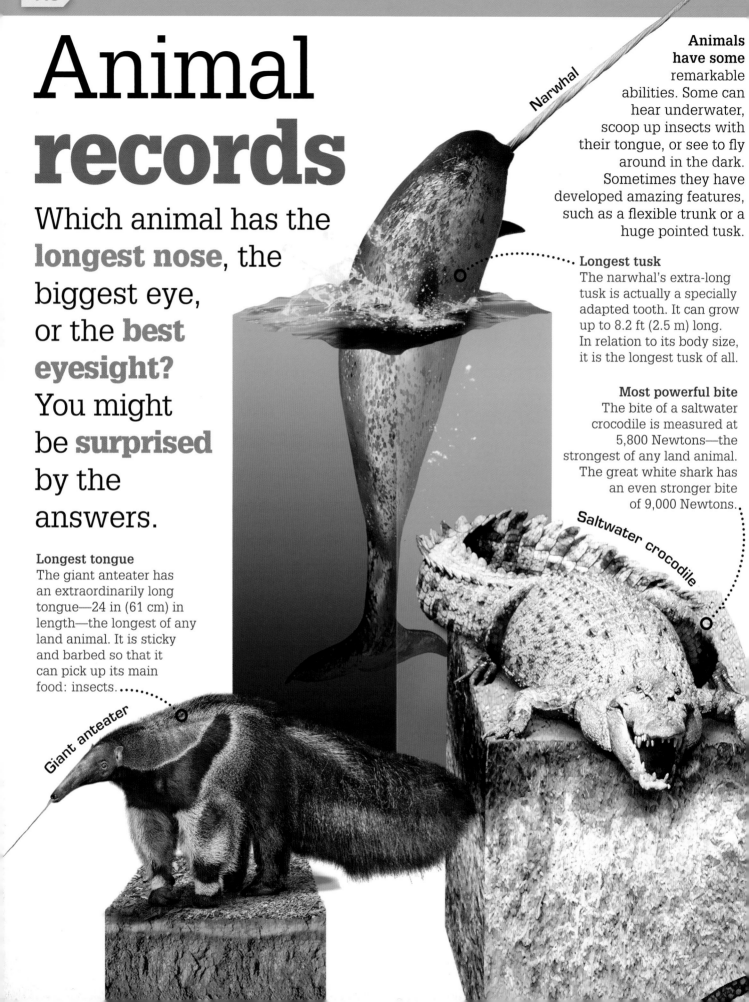

Narwhal

Saltwater crocodile

Giant anteater

Widest hearing range
A porpoise has a wide hearing range—up to 150,000 kHz (kilohertz), a dog up to 46,000 kHz, and a human up to 20,000 kHz. Fish such as the American shad have a range up to 180 kHz to stay one step ahead of predatory porpoise.

Porpoise

Longest nose
The African elephant's trunk is the longest nose in the animal kingdom. In addition to being sensitive enough to pick up small items and strong enough to bat away a lion, it can detect a huge range of scents.

Elephant trunk

Best insect night vision
This bee—the nocturnal carpenter bee—can fly at night and still find food and pick out colors, even when there is no moon. Nocturnal hawk moths can also see colors at night.

Carpenter bees

The African elephant **also has** the largest ears—**more than 3.3 ft (1 m) long.**

Biggest eye
Colossal squid are huge creatures so it's not surprising that their eyes are the largest in the animal kingdom. Each eye measures about 11 in (28 cm) in diameter—about the same as a dinner plate.

Colossal squid

Life in the **fast** lane

Meet the **speediest** creatures on **land**, in **water**, and in the **air**. In a head-to-head (or wing-to-tail) **race**, which one runs away with **gold**?

15 mph
(24.5 km/h)

Elephant

27.8 mph
(44.7 km/h)

Athlete

If **people** ran as fast as **cheetahs**, the **100-m** record would be **3.6 seconds**.

Dolphin

18.6 mph
(30 km/h)

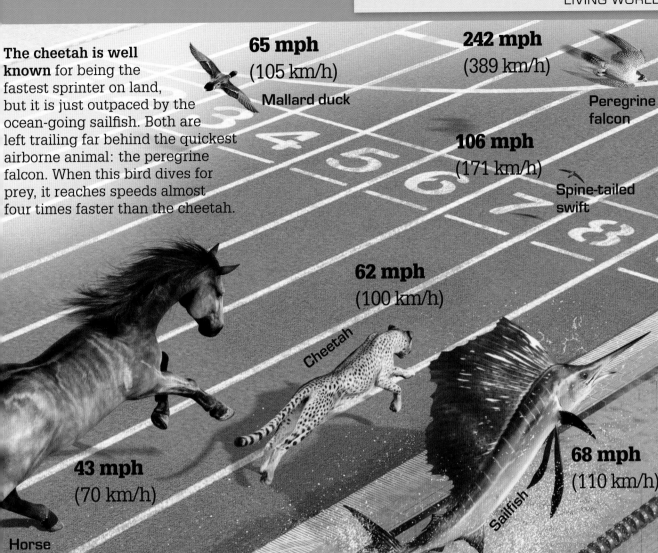

The cheetah is well known for being the fastest sprinter on land, but it is just outpaced by the ocean-going sailfish. Both are left trailing far behind the quickest airborne animal: the peregrine falcon. When this bird dives for prey, it reaches speeds almost four times faster than the cheetah.

65 mph (105 km/h)
Mallard duck

242 mph (389 km/h)
Peregrine falcon

106 mph (171 km/h)
Spine-tailed swift

62 mph (100 km/h)
Cheetah

68 mph (110 km/h)
Sailfish

43 mph (70 km/h)
Horse

FAST FACTS

Stamina and a long stride can often beat sprinting. Pronghorn antelopes can outrun cheetahs over long distances.

Pronghorns are the fastest animal over distance, reaching 35 mph (56 km/h) over 4 miles (6 km). They have a sprint speed of 55 mph (88.5 km/h), and a 29-ft (9-m) stride.

Ostriches are the fastest animal on two legs, sprinting at 45 mph (72 km/h) and maintaining a speed of 25 mph (40 km/h) over 1.2 miles (2 km).

FAST FACTS

The largest bird, the ostrich, also lays the largest egg. One example weighed 91.35 oz (2.59 kg). The smallest egg is laid by a vervain hummingbird, and it weighs less than 0.01 oz (0.36 g). A medium-sized chicken's egg, by comparison, weighs 1.87 oz (53 g).

Hummingbird egg

Chicken egg

Ostrich egg

Most talkative
The African grey parrot is a great talker; it can learn as many as 1,000 words.

Smallest bird
The tiny bee hummingbird is the smallest bird. It is just 2 in (5–6 cm) long.

Largest bird
The ostrich can grow up to 9 ft (2.8 m) tall—making it the biggest bird of all. It's also the fastest bird on land—capable of running at speeds of 45 mph (72 km/h).

Brilliant birds

Birds can **soar in the skies** and **race** along the ground. Some have **huge beaks** for catching fish, while others are so tiny they collect **nectar** from flowers.

Longest wingspan
These enormous wings belong to a wandering albatross. The wings stretch for 8.2 ft–11.5 ft (2.5–3.5 m) and help the albatross glide effortlessly along on currents of air.

Longest beak
The bird with the longest beak is the Australian pelican. Its bill can be up to 18 in (47 cm) long— that's as long as three hot dogs!

Oldest bird
Is this the oldest bird ever? It's certainly the oldest flamingo. Named "Greater," this flamingo lived in Adelaide Zoo, Australia, until it was 83 years old.

A wandering albatross **was recorded flying 3,700 miles (6,000 km) in 12 days.**

BIRDS OF A FEATHER

This spectacular display of bright green budgerigars takes place over the grassland of central Australia. Up to 10,000 birds swoop down each morning looking for water, forming the largest collection of budgerigars in the world. They pause for a few seconds to drink before taking off again.

Longest migration on land
Caribou, also known as reindeer, living in North America, travel south when winter approaches to escape the extreme cold. They spend the winter months in forests and head north again to breed, making a total trip of 1,860 miles (3,000 km), marked by the purple arrow on this map.

GLOBE-TROTTERS

Millions of globe skimmer dragonflies are believed to leave India and fly over the sea to Africa each year. The whole journey of about 11,100 miles (18,000 km) is not made by individual dragonflies but by four generations, with the insects stopping off on islands to breed and lay eggs en route.

A great white shark was recorded making a trip of 12,500 miles (20,000 km).

Longest migration by sea
After feeding in polar waters during the summer, humpback whales travel to tropical waters to give birth to their young. The whales and their calves head back to the poles to feed again, making a round-trip of up to 10,000 miles (16,000 km), shown by the blue arrows on the map. Gray whales may make even longer migrations.

FAST FACTS

Atlantic salmon have a remarkable life cycle. Each fish migrates from the river where it was born out to sea. Once they are adults, they make their way back to the same river where they were born to breed and lay their eggs. Then they return to the ocean.

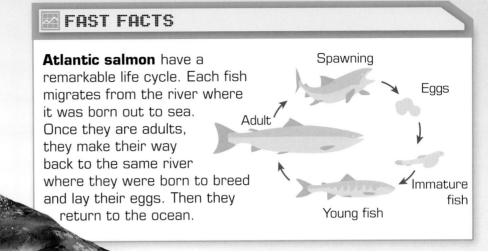

Spawning

Eggs

Adult

Immature fish

Young fish

Many animals, especially birds, migrate away from the winter cold. They often set off in groups and follow the same route every year, the young learning the way from their parents.

Longest migration by air
The Arctic tern is a remarkable bird, it makes the longest migration of any animal. Each year it spends the northern summer in the Arctic then flies to the Antarctic for the southern summer, before returning to the Arctic again— a round-trip of 46,600 miles (75,000 km)— shown by the red arrow on the map.

A long way to go

Every year, **huge numbers** of animals set off on **long journeys** in search of food, a mate, or warmer climes. In addition to being long, these **migrations** are **hazardous**.

Giants
of the deep

The **blue whale** is well known as the **world's biggest** animal, but how do other large **sea creatures** measure up?

Lion's mane jellyfish tentacles are longer than a blue whale.

Largest jellyfish: Lion's mane jellyfish
7.5 ft (2.3 m) wide

The jellyfish's bell (body) may be large, but it's no comparison to its longest tentacles, which can stretch for 120 ft (36.5 m).

World's largest-ever animal: Blue whale
107 ft (32.6 m)

The water in the oceans supports the weight of an animal's body, which helps them to grow to sizes that wouldn't be possible on land. An average blue whale weighs 30 times more than an elephant—no legs could stand up to that!

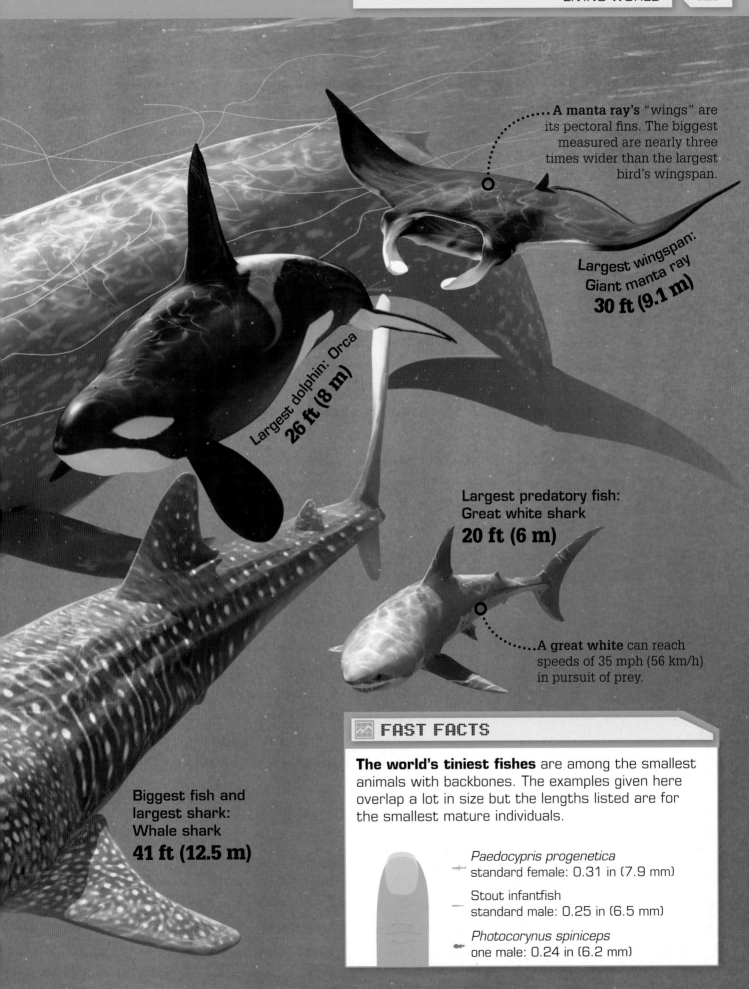

A manta ray's "wings" are its pectoral fins. The biggest measured are nearly three times wider than the largest bird's wingspan.

Largest wingspan:
Giant manta ray
30 ft (9.1 m)

Largest dolphin: Orca
26 ft (8 m)

Largest predatory fish:
Great white shark
20 ft (6 m)

A great white can reach speeds of 35 mph (56 km/h) in pursuit of prey.

Biggest fish and
largest shark:
Whale shark
41 ft (12.5 m)

FAST FACTS

The world's tiniest fishes are among the smallest animals with backbones. The examples given here overlap a lot in size but the lengths listed are for the smallest mature individuals.

Paedocypris progenetica
standard female: 0.31 in (7.9 mm)

Stout infantfish
standard male: 0.25 in (6.5 mm)

Photocorynus spiniceps
one male: 0.24 in (6.2 mm)

Mini**beasts**

These **mighty minibeasts** might not be welcome at your next picnic. They are some of the **heavyweights and giants** of the insect world.

Fastest flyer
When a horsefly is in pursuit of a mate, it has been known to reach speeds of 90 mph (145 km/h).

Largest caterpillar
At 6 in (15 cm) in length, the hickory horned devil caterpillar is almost as long as a banana. Even though it looks scary, its spikes do not sting.

Longest insect
This very long stick insect—*Phryganistria chinensis Zhao*—measuring 24.5 in (62.4 cm) was discovered in southern China in 2014. The measurements are from the tip of its front legs to the tip of its back legs.

Longest beetle
The Hercules beetle is an impressive creature from the rain forests of Central and South America. It can reach 6.7 in (17 cm) in length and lift 17 lb (8 kg)—that is 80 times its own weight.

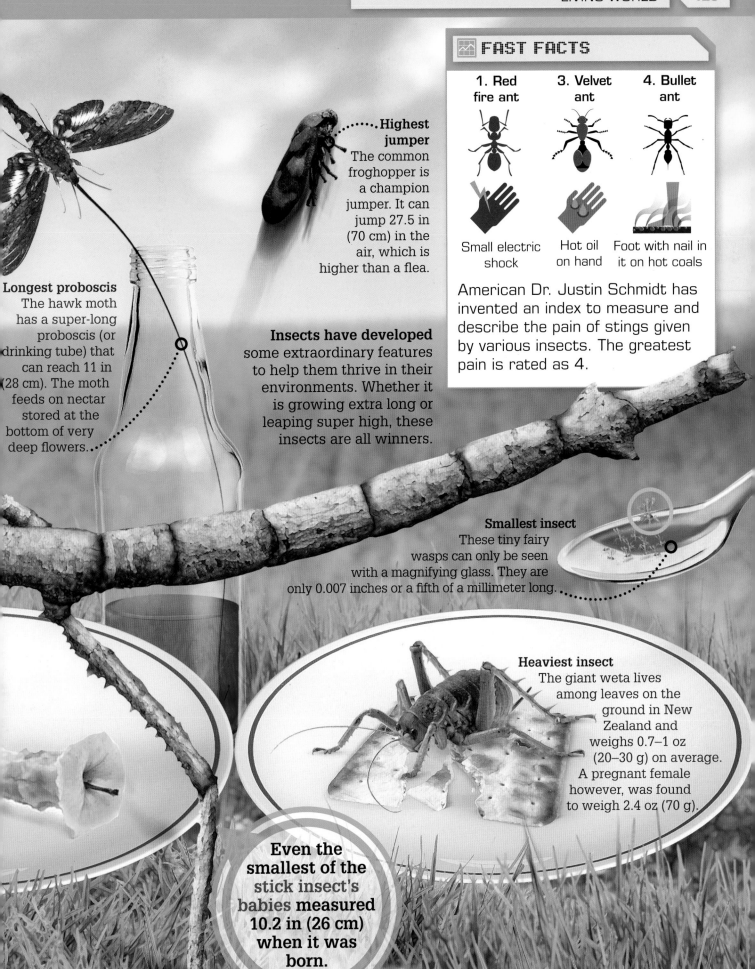

Highest jumper
The common froghopper is a champion jumper. It can jump 27.5 in (70 cm) in the air, which is higher than a flea.

FAST FACTS

1. Red fire ant

Small electric shock

3. Velvet ant

Hot oil on hand

4. Bullet ant

Foot with nail in it on hot coals

American Dr. Justin Schmidt has invented an index to measure and describe the pain of stings given by various insects. The greatest pain is rated as 4.

Longest proboscis
The hawk moth has a super-long proboscis (or drinking tube) that can reach 11 in (28 cm). The moth feeds on nectar stored at the bottom of very deep flowers.

Insects have developed some extraordinary features to help them thrive in their environments. Whether it is growing extra long or leaping super high, these insects are all winners.

Smallest insect
These tiny fairy wasps can only be seen with a magnifying glass. They are only 0.007 inches or a fifth of a millimeter long.

Heaviest insect
The giant weta lives among leaves on the ground in New Zealand and weighs 0.7–1 oz (20–30 g) on average. A pregnant female however, was found to weigh 2.4 oz (70 g).

Even the smallest of the stick insect's babies measured 10.2 in (26 cm) when it was born.

Longest snake
The world's
longest snake is the
reticulated python.
There are reports of
it reaching lengths
of 32 ft (10 m),
though it's usually
nearer to 23 ft (7 m).

Most venomous
Look out for this
snake because its
bite is lethal. The
inland taipan lives
in Australia and is
the most venomous
snake in the world,
just one bite could
kill 100 adult men.

Longest fangs
Lurking in the rain
forests and savannas
of central Africa,
the Gaboon viper
has the longest
fangs of all
snakes—
they are 2 in
(5 cm) long.

Smallest snake
This tiny snake is only 4 in
(10 cm) long and as thin as a
spaghetti strand. It is called
a Barbados threadsnake.

Super snakes

Some snakes are **many feet long**; others can give a **deadly bite** with their **needlelike fangs**. However, most won't attack unless they are disturbed.

The black mamba is not actually black—except for the inside of its mouth.

Fastest snake
The black mamba, found in Africa, is highly venomous and can also move super fast. It has been known to reach speeds of more than 6.8 mph (11 km/h), making it a terrifying predator.

Snakes vary in size from pythons as thick as your forearm to noodlethin threadsnakes. There are also fierce snakes with long fangs that can give a nasty bite.

FAST FACTS

The green anaconda is the heaviest snake in the world, weighing a massive 500 lb (227 kg). That's as much as two and a half male red kangaroos, which weigh 198 lb (90 kg) each.

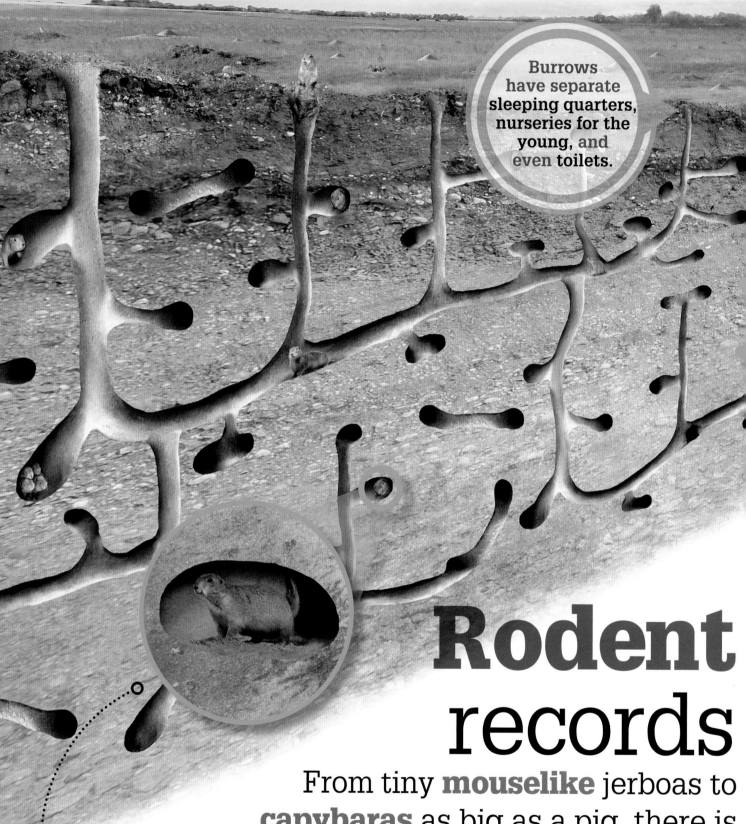

Burrows have separate sleeping quarters, nurseries for the young, and even toilets.

Rodent records

From tiny **mouselike** jerboas to **capybaras** as big as a pig, there is a wide variety of **rodents**. Some dig vast **burrows** underground to live in and raise their young.

Largest prairie dog town
A network of prairie dog burrows in Texas covered 25,000 sq miles (65,000 sq km). That's the size of the state of West Virginia or the country of Lithuania. It was home for 400 million prairie dogs.

Highest-jumping rodent
This kangaroo rat can leap up to 9 ft (2.75 m) high. It has extra-long back legs and weighs less than 4.5 oz (128 g).

Spikiest rodent
Porcupines have long spines called quills to protect them from predators. The quills of the North African crested porcupine can be up to 13.7 in (35 cm) long.

Smallest rodent
The tiny Asian Baluchistan pygmy jerboa measures just 1.7 in (4.4 cm) from its head to the start of its tail—its tail is 3 in (8 cm) long.

Biggest rodent
The capybara spends a lot of time in water in its South American habitat. It grows to 53 in (134 cm) long and weighs up to 145 lb (66 kg).

Biggest ears
With a body just 3.7 in (9.5 cm) long and ears measuring 1.5–2 in (4–5 cm) in length, the long-eared jerboa is appropriately named. It has the longest ears compared to its body of any mammal.

Rodents are mammals with two continuously growing teeth, which they use to eat plants and seeds. Some also have an extra-long tail to help them balance when they jump.

BIGGEST TEETH

The largest rodent that has ever lived was the *Josephoartigasia monesi*. This creature, which was the size of a bull, lived during the Pliocene period (2.6–5.3 million years ago). It was about 5 ft (1.5 m) tall and 10 ft (3 m) long and had enormous incisor teeth that were 12 in (30 cm) long. It probably used its teeth for digging and fighting as well as eating.

Most like humans
Both chimpanzees and bonobos (an ape that looks very similar to the chimpanzee) share 98.7 percent of their DNA with humans.

Smallest ape
Though gibbons are the smallest apes—about 3.2 ft (1 m) tall—they have the longest arms in relation to their body of any animal.

Largest ape
The mighty Eastern gorilla is the largest of the apes. Males grow up to 6 ft (1.9 m) tall and can weigh 461 lb (209 kg).

A gibbon **can reach speeds of 35 mph (56 km/h) when it swings through the trees.**

Most intelligent
Studies have found that the orangutan may be the most intelligent ape. They can use a variety of tools and spend many years educating their young.

Apes and monkeys are both primates, but apes are bigger and, unlike most monkeys, do not have tails. Apes are more intelligent and more likely to use tools to get their food. Monkeys live in all sorts of environments, including snowy ones.

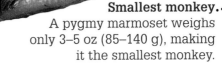

Loudest monkey
The howler monkey makes deep, booming calls that can be heard up to 3 miles (5 km) away.

Smallest monkey
A pygmy marmoset weighs only 3–5 oz (85–140 g), making it the smallest monkey.

Longest nose
The proboscis monkey has the longest nose (or proboscis). It is so long that the monkey has to push it aside to eat.

Largest monkey
The mandrill is the largest monkey, growing up to 2.6 ft (80 cm) tall and weighing 73 lb (33 kg). However, it is nowhere near as big as the largest ape. It is the most distinctive monkey, though, with its red nose and blue face patches.

Most northerly monkey
The Japanese macaque lives the furthest north of any nonhuman primate, dwelling in snowy landscapes where temperatures can reach as low as 5°F (–15°C).

Prize-winning
primates

Our nearest relatives, **apes and monkeys** are **intelligent** animals, but which are the largest, the **loudest**, or the most like us?

Big babies

From the **tallest newborns** to **super-sized litters** and long **pregnancies**, discover these record-breaking **mammal** babies.

A newborn giraffe is on its feet within 20 minutes of being born.

All the babies here are placental **mammals**, which means that they develop fully inside their mother. Marsupial mammals, such as kangaroos, have young that continue to develop in their mother's pouch after birth.

Most babies
A female rabbit in the wild can have 360 kits in her lifetime, up to 14 in each litter.

Tallest baby
A newborn giraffe is 6 ft (1.8 m) tall—the same height as an average adult man.

Biggest litter
Tenrecs—small, hedgehoglike animals from Madagascar— have up to 32 babies in one litter. The average litter size is 18.

WEIGHTY WHALES

The heaviest newborn of all is the 23-ft (7-m) long blue whale, weighing in at 6,000 lb (2,700 kg). This is 66 times lighter than its mother—in fact, it's the same weight as her tongue.

Smallest baby compared to mother At birth, a panda cub is 900 times smaller than its mother by weight. A human baby is about 20 times smaller than its mom.

Longest childhood
A female orangutan is looked after by its mother for eight years, the longest care in the animal kingdom.

Longest pregnancy
A baby elephant takes 640–660 days (22 months) to develop inside its mother. That's more than twice as long as a human baby's 280 days (9 months).

Longest life spans

Life can be fleeting or long-lasting in the **animal kingdom**. Some creatures pack a lifetime into a **day**, while others can survive for **centuries**.

Mayfly (1 day)
Some mayflies live for a few hours or days, but one species lives for less than 5 minutes—just long enough to mate and lay eggs.

Asian elephant (86 years)
Apart from humans, the longest-living land mammal is the mighty elephant. An Asian elephant named Lin Wang lived to be 86 years old in Taipei Zoo, Taiwan.

Humans (up to 122 years)
We are the longest-living, land-dwelling mammals on Earth, with the oldest person ever reaching 122 years.

Bowhead whale (more than 200 years)
Bowhead whales are the longest-living mammals in the sea (and on land), capable of reaching 211 years of age.

200

100

Aldabra giant tortoise (255 years)
The oldest reptile ever recorded lived in Kolkata, India. The Aldabra giant tortoise named Adwaita reached 255 years of age. It died in 1965.

Koi carp (226 years)
This popular pet species can live a long life. A koi carp named Hanako was reported to be 226 years old when she died in 1977.

250

300

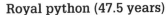

Naked mole rat (28 years)
This strange-looking underground rodent from East Africa is the longest-living rodent, capable of reaching 28 years of age.

Royal python (47.5 years)
The longest-living snake is the nonvenomous royal python from Africa. It is a popular pet and can live for more than 47 years in captivity.

There are big differences in the life spans of animals, though they all face the same challenges to survive. They must hunt for food, avoid predators, and find a mate in order to produce the next generation.

30

Laysan albatross (67 years)
The oldest bird recorded in the wild is a 67-year-old Laysan albatross named Wisdom.

Termite queen (50 years)
The termite queen can live for 50 years, making her the world's longest-living insect.

50

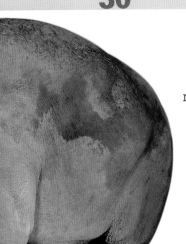

60

Greenland shark (392 years)
Researchers have found a Greenland shark aged about 392 years old, making her the longest-living vertebrate.

Icelandic clam (507 years)
Meet Hafrún, the Icelandic clam aged 507 years old. This ocean quahog holds the record for the longest-living mollusk.

Deep sea sponges **including** *Monorhaphis chuni* **are estimated to live for 11,000 years.**

500

11,000

Animal data

THE BIG SLEEP

DALL'S PORPOISE POSSIBLY NO SLEEP

LITTLE BROWN BAT

THE **LITTLE BROWN BAT** SLEEPS FOR ALMOST **20 HOURS A DAY.** SOME ANIMALS, SUCH AS **DALL'S PORPOISE,** APPEAR **NOT TO SLEEP AT ALL.**

19.9 HOURS

THE **EDIBLE DORMOUSE** HAS THE **LONGEST HIBERNATION** OF ANY ANIMAL: MORE THAN 11 MONTHS OF THE YEAR.

1	2	3	4
5	6	7	8
9	10	11	12

mini MALS

SMALLEST MAMMAL: KITTI'S HOG-NOSED BAT, 1.2 IN (30 MM) BODY LENGTH

SMALLEST REPTILE: BROOKESIA MICRA CHAMELEON, 1.1 IN (29 MM) FROM NOSE TO TAIL

SMALLEST AMPHIBIAN: PAEDOPHRYNE AMAUENSIS FROG, 0.3 IN (7.7 MM) LONG

SMALLEST INVERTEBRATE: TINY AQUATIC CREATURES CALLED ROTIFERS ARE AMONG THE SMALLEST ANIMALS. THE TINIEST IS 0.002 IN (0.05 MM) LONG.

IT'S A KNOCKOUT

Peacock mantis shrimps have one of the **fastest and most powerful punches** made by any animal, striking with a force **2,500 times their own body weight** in less than 800 microseconds (0.0008 seconds). They use **special clubs** on their front legs to **smash the shells of crabs** for food. The force of their **punch is so great** that it has been known to **smash the glass of an aquarium**.

POW

DEADLIEST **CREATURES**

CASSOWARIES HAVE THE LONGEST CLAWS: THE DAGGERLIKE INNER TOE CAN BE 5 IN (12.5 CM) LONG.

ANOPHELES MOSQUITOES ARE THE DEADLIEST ANIMALS OF ALL: FEMALE MOSQUITOES SPREAD MALARIA THROUGH THEIR BITES, KILLING HUNDREDS OF THOUSANDS OF PEOPLE EVERY YEAR.

SPERM WHALES HAVE THE BIGGEST TEETH OF ANY PREDATOR: UP TO 8 IN (20 CM) LONG.

ELECTRIC EELS HAVE THE STRONGEST ELECTRICAL DISCHARGE: EACH SHOCK CAN PROVIDE 600 VOLTS OF POWER. THAT'S NEARLY THREE TIMES THE VOLTAGE PROVIDED BY A HOUSEHOLD ELECTRIC SOCKET.

MEGA MUNCHERS

The **blue whale** eats the **most food of any animal**: around **6 tons of krill**—or **40 million** of the **tiny sea crustaceans**—every day. That's **about 4–5 percent** of its **body weight.**

LONGEST **ANIMAL**

A **bootlace worm** measuring more than **180 ft (55 m) long** washed up from the **North Sea** onto the coast of **Scotland, UK, in 1864.** Stretched out, it could wrap around the **edge of these pages** more than **80 times**.

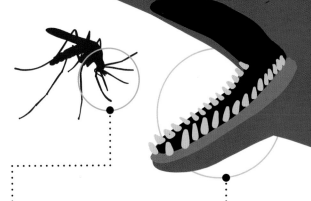

125%

4–5%

Eurasian pygmy shrews eat **125 percent** of their **body weight a day**: that's up to **0.18 oz (5 g) of food a day.**

FAST FACTS

Dinosaur brains were much smaller than those of modern-day mammals. *Troodon* was the smartest, with a brain and body size similar to an ostrich, but *Stegosaurus*'s brain was the size of a lime, which was tiny for a dinosaur that grew to 30 ft (9 m) long.

Troodon

Stegosaurus

Biggest wings
Quetzalcoatlus had a whopping wingspan of more than 33 ft (10 m), so this reptile was the largest flying animal ever known.

Biggest dinosaur
Argentinosaurus measured 98 ft (30 m) long and weighed more than 60 tons, making it one of the largest land animals to have ever lived. However, the very similar *Patagotitan* may have been even bigger.

Largest head
Heads don't come bigger than this! A *Pentaceratops* skull measuring 9.8 ft (3 m) crowned it the largest head of any land animal.

Longest tail
Diplodocus had the longest tail of any dinosaur, measuring up to 43 ft (13 m) long.

Awesome dinosaurs

Size matters for dinosaurs. Although these extinct reptiles lived more than **66 million years ago**, they are still the **largest creatures** to have ever walked the Earth.

Longest neck
Plant-munching *Mamenchisaurus* from China had a neck stretching 32 ft (10 m) long, which was half the dinosaur's total length.

Mighty *Mamenchisaurus* had a neck almost as long as a school bus!

Longest claws
Therizinosaurus waved the biggest claws, with three curved blades measuring 30 in (76 cm) on each hand.

Dinosaurs ruled the world for 160 million years. Thanks to discoveries of their fossilized remains, experts have identified more than 1,000 species. Among them are the biggest, longest, and heaviest dinosaurs, producing the animal kingdom's most mind-blowing measurements.

The **dinosaur** tail continues...

From the **first to the fastest**, and the **latest to the longest-lived**, these dinosaurs have all broken records. However, the story is not finished—**fossils** are still being found bringing new information and new records.

First dinosaur
Fossils of this small, dog-sized dinosaur, named *Nyasasaurus parringtoni*, were uncovered in Tanzania. They have been dated at 243 million years old, which is more than 10 million years earlier than any other dinosaur fossils....

The story of dinosaurs still presents us with some puzzles. Here are some of the earliest dinosaurs that have been discovered as well as some that survived for the longest.

Diplodocus **had a long digestive system** to help it digest its **fibrous, leafy diet**.

A record-breaking collection of dinosaur eggs is housed at the Heyuan Museum in Guangdong Province, China. More than 10,000 eggs are on display dating from the late Cretaceous period, which was approximately 65—89 million years ago.

Longest-lived dinosaur
Diplodocus, like other sauropods (long-necked, plant-eating dinosaurs), had a life as long as its neck. Sauropods were among the longest-lived dinosaurs, surviving for up to 80 years.

First-named dinosaur
Megalosaurus was the first dinosaur to be named. In 1924, British geologist, Reverend William Buckland, found the fossil remains and gave the dinosaur its name, which means "great lizard."

Most recent dinosaur
This dinosaur was a survivor. Fossils of the plant-eating *hadrosaurs* have been dated at 64.5 million years. If the date is right, this means it survived the huge asteroid that killed off the large dinosaurs and was still around 700,000 years later.

Fastest dinosaur
The *ornithomimids* were the speediest dinosaurs. They looked a bit like big birds with feathers, beaks, and long legs. *Struthiomimus* had a top speed of 45 mph (72 km/h).

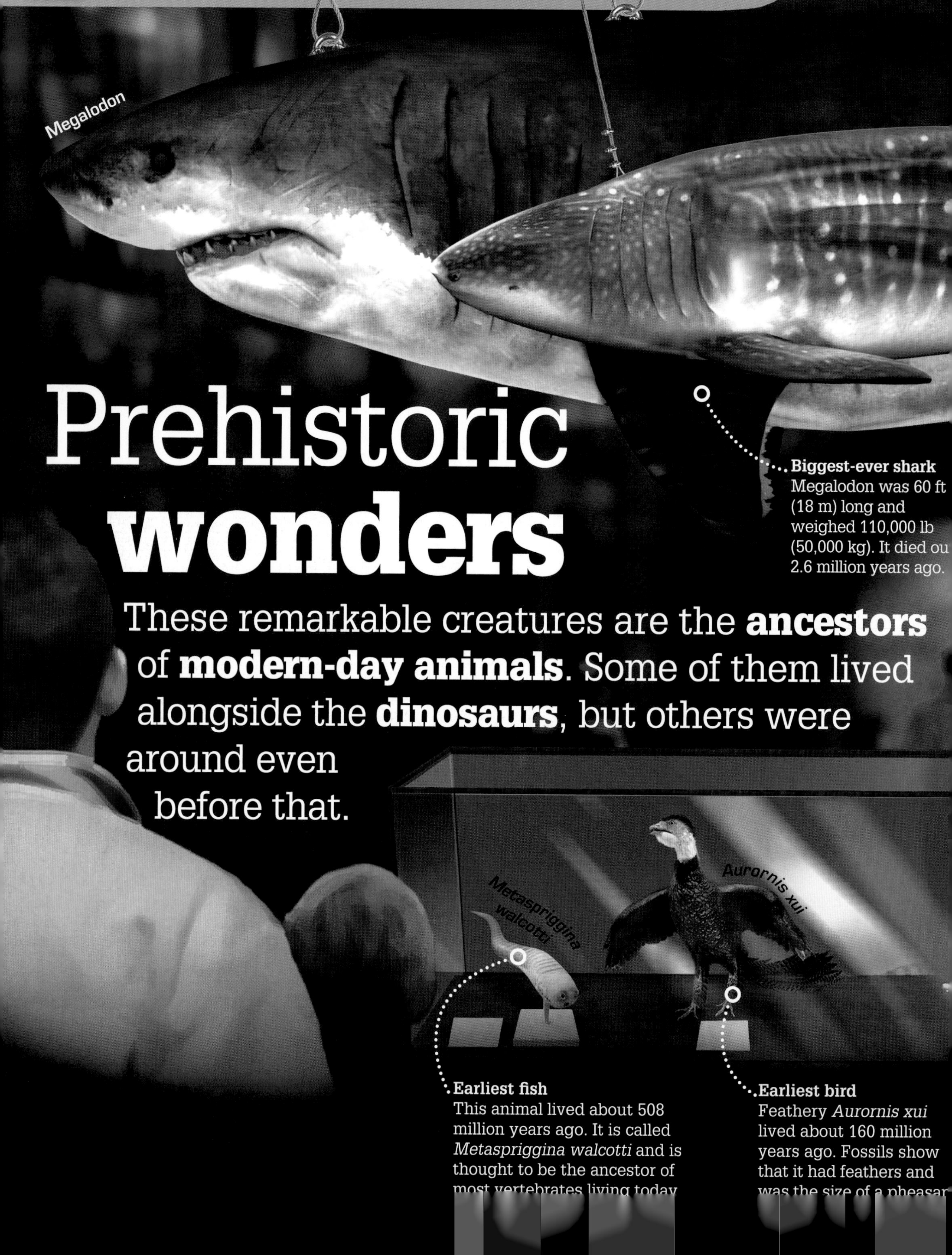

Megalodon

Prehistoric
wonders

These remarkable creatures are the **ancestors** of **modern-day animals**. Some of them lived alongside the **dinosaurs**, but others were around even before that.

Biggest-ever shark
Megalodon was 60 ft (18 m) long and weighed 110,000 lb (50,000 kg). It died ou 2.6 million years ago.

Metaspriggina walcotti

Aurornis xui

Earliest fish
This animal lived about 508 million years ago. It is called *Metaspriggina walcotti* and is thought to be the ancestor of most vertebrates living today

Earliest bird
Feathery *Aurornis xui* lived about 160 million years ago. Fossils show that it had feathers and was the size of a pheasan

Whale shark

Biggest shark today
The largest shark alive today is the whale shark. On average, whale sharks are 32.8 ft (10 m) long.

Paraceratherium

Biggest land mammal
The *Paraceratherium* was the largest land mammal and ancestor of the modern-day rhinoceros (though it didn't have a horn). It weighed 44,000 lb (20,000 kg) and was 18 ft (5.5 m) tall...

FAST FACTS

The ancestors of the elephant are the mammoths, including the woolly mammoth that lived in Russia, especially Siberia, and North America until 4,300 years ago. The mastodons are more distantly related to elephants and roamed North America until 10,000 years ago.

American mastodon

Woolly mammoth

African elephant

White rhinoceros

These are some of the ancestors of modern-day animals. They look a bit like animals we know, though some were much, much bigger.

Juramaia

Earliest mammal
This shrewlike creature was found in Liaoning Province, China. It is the earliest example of a placental mammal—an animal that gives birth to live, more developed young.

Biggest rhino
The white rhinoceros is the largest of the five rhino species and the second-largest land mammal; African and Asian elephants are the largest.

A *Tyrannosaurus* named **Sue**

In 1990, in South Dakota, **paleontologist Sue Hendrickson** spotted the fossils of a gigantic *Tyrannosaurus rex*. The dinosaur was named Sue after her, and it turned out to be a record breaker.

The skull
Sue's massive skull weighs about 600 lb (270 kg) and includes 58 daggerlike teeth.

Fossils were found of more than 90 per cent of this *T.rex* skeleton.

 **FAST FACTS**

The titanosaurs include the largest dinosaurs ever found—as well as the *Tyrannosaurus*. *Patagotitan* is a titanosaur that was discovered in Argentina in 2012. Its thigh bone is the largest fossil discovered, measuring 7.8 ft (2.4 m) long. The fossils are on display in the American Museum of Natural History, New York.

Patagotitan
122 ft (37 m) long

Sue 40.4 ft
(12.3 m) long

Human
6 ft
(1.8 m) tall

Patagotitan
thigh bone
7.8 ft (2.4 m) long

Largest and most complete
Sue measures 40.4 ft (12.3 m) from snout to tail and contains 250 bones and teeth. It is the most complete *T. rex* ever found.

Most valuable
This *T. rex* skeleton is also the world's most valuable. At an auction in 1997, it was sold to the Field Museum, Chicago, for $8.36 million (£6 million).

Sue, the *Tyrannosaurus rex*, stands guard in the Field Museum, Chicago, where it attracts many visitors. It took more than 30,000 hours to prepare the fossil skeleton before it was put on display here.

Tree-mendous

The first trees grew on Earth about **385 million years ago.** Today, there are **3 trillion** trees providing a **life-support system** for our planet, bringing **oxygen** and **shelter** for animals, including humans.

Widest tree

The world's widest tree is *El Arbol del Tule*, a Montezuma cypress in Mexico, reaching more than 30 ft (9 m) across. It was mistaken for a group of trees at first because it is so wide. It would take 17 people with their arms outstretched to reach around the vast trunk.

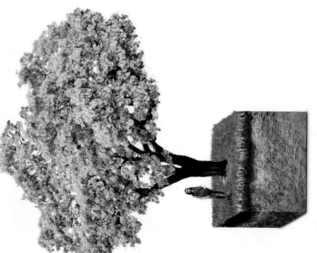

Fastest-growing tree

China's empress tree is the world's fastest-growing tree. In one year, it grows 20 ft (6 m) in height—that's about 12 in (30 cm) every few weeks. The empress breaks another record, too—it produces at least three times more oxygen than any other type of tree.

Hyperion is such a giant that the tiny human figures in its branches look like insects on a garden plant!

Oldest tree

The oldest trees still growing today are the bristlecone pines in the White Mountains of California. Their growth rings reveal that they are more than 9,000 years old.

Rarest tree

There is only one *Pennantia baylisiana* growing anywhere in the wild. This solitary tree can be found on one of the Three Kings Islands off New Zealand.

Trees are natural wonders, whether growing in forests or alone on mountainsides. Some trees have survived for thousands of years, and others have grown to dizzying heights.

FAST FACTS

A study in 2015 estimated that there were 3 trillion trees on Earth. Russia has the most trees with 642 billion, followed by Canada (318 billion), Brazil (302 billion), and the US (228 billion).

Russia 642 billion

Canada 318 billion

Brazil 302 billion

US 228 billion

Tallest tree

The world's tallest tree is mighty Hyperion, standing 380 ft (116 m) tall when it was measured in Redwood National Park in California, in 2006. Very few people know the exact location of this record-breaking redwood.

Oldest root system

Old Tjikko is a Norway spruce in the Fulufjället Mountains of Sweden. It has a root system that is about 9,550 years old.

Hyperion is 75.5 ft (23 m) taller than the Statue of Liberty.

Flower power

Flowers have been growing on Earth for more than **150 million years**. Explore these blooms and discover nature's most impressive flowers, from the **biggest blossom** to the **stinkiest flowers**.

Biggest flower
The world's most gigantic flower is Indonesia's *Rafflesia arnoldii*, which can grow to 3.3 ft (1 m) wide and weigh 22 lb (10 kg).

Both the largest and tallest flowers are among the stinkiest! *Rafflesia arnoldii* and titan arum are called "corpse flowers" because they smell of rotten meat.

Short-lived flowers
South America's kadupul cactus flower is a rare sight. White flowers with a beautiful scent appear only at night and are dead by morning. An orchid called *Dendrobium appendiculatum* opens for only five minutes.

**Tallest, smelliest
flowering structure**
The spike of a titan arum
grows up to 9.8 ft
(3 m) tall and is covered
with tiny flowers. It
grows in the steamy
rain forests of Indonesia.

Slowest growing
The Bolivian bromeliad
Puya raimondii is the
ultimate late developer.
Flowers first appear
between 80 and 150
years after this plant
starts growing!

FAST FACTS

The world's tiniest flower
blooms on the super-small *Wolffia
globosa*, more commonly known
as the Asian watermeal. Found
floating in streams and ponds,
the whole plant measures only
0.02 in (0.6 mm) long and
0.01 in (0.3 mm) wide—about
the same size as a grain of salt.

Oldest flowers
Some of the oldest
known flowering plants
found as fossils lived
in water, such as
this *Archaefructus*.
The oldest, named
Montsechia, dates back
to 130 million years.

Most expensive flowering plant
The Shenzhen Nongke orchid
took eight years to produce in
a laboratory before being sold
at auction in 2005 for a record-
breaking $202,000 (£144,000).

Leafy legends

It's not only a plant's **flowers** that attract attention. Leaves can also grow to **extraordinary lengths** and survive in **water**, in the **desert**, or at the very tops of trees.

⊠ FAST FACTS

Coconut trees are probably the most useful trees in the world. Their leaves are woven into baskets, wood is used for building and carved into utensils, fiber is turned into ropes and matting, coconuts are eaten, and their oil is used as flavoring and in cosmetics.

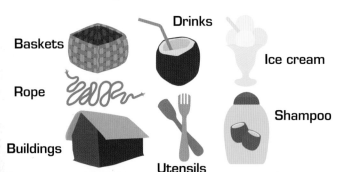

Baskets

Rope

Buildings

Drinks

Ice cream

Utensils

Shampoo

Biggest floating leaf
Victoria amazonica water lily leaves can reach 10 ft (3 m) in diameter. They are so strong, they can support the weight of a small child.

Longest vine

This twisting vine is an elephant creeper, a type of liana (a woody vine that grows up from the ground and wraps itself around trees). It was claimed that one specimen in India reached 4,900 ft (1.5 km) in length.

Tallest cactus

The tallest-ever cactus was a species of cardon, or elephant cactus. Growing in Mexico's Sonora Desert, it topped 63 ft (19.2 m)—that's taller than 10 men standing on each other's shoulders.

Fastest-growing plant

Bamboos include some of the fastest-growing plants. One species has been recorded growing 35 in (91 cm) in a day—so fast you can actually see it. In a year, it grows 1,090 ft (332.38 m).

Longest leaf

The plant with the longest leaf is the *Raphia regalis*, a type of raffia palm with leaves that can grow up to 82 ft (25 m) long—that's taller than the tree's 69-ft (21-m) height.

Most poisonous plant

The seeds of the castor bean contain ricin, a deadly toxin that is 12,000 times more poisonous than rattlesnake venom.

Plants can thrive in all sorts of environments. Their leaves are their food factories, absorbing light and producing sugar to give the plant energy to grow. The bigger the leaf, the more food it can make.

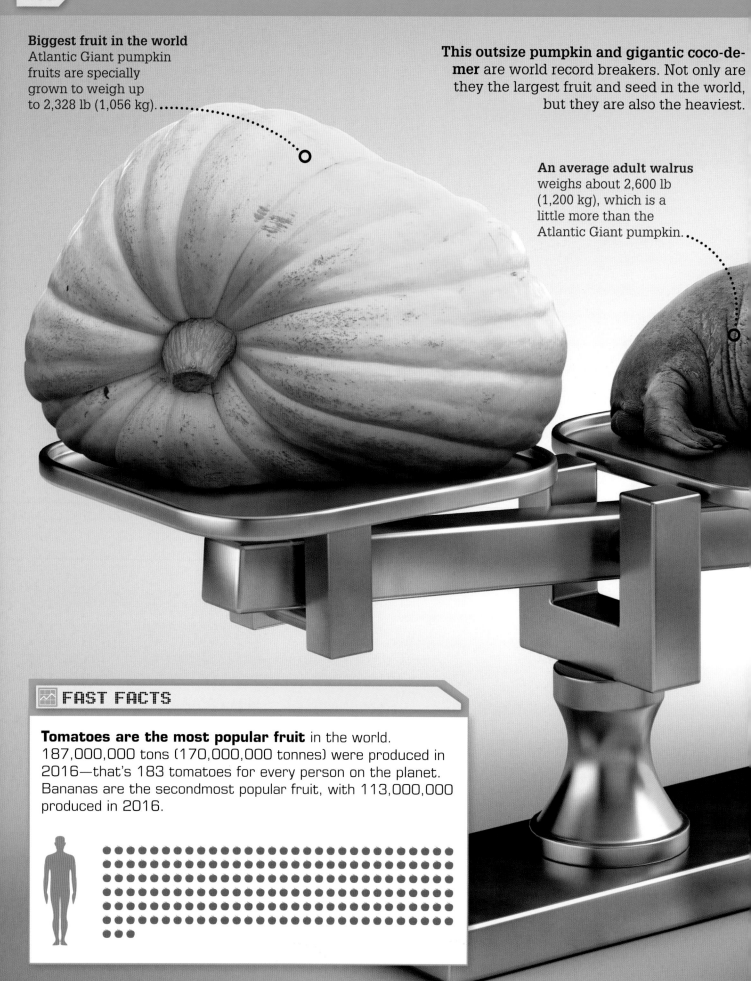

Biggest fruit in the world
Atlantic Giant pumpkin fruits are specially grown to weigh up to 2,328 lb (1,056 kg).

This outsize pumpkin and gigantic coco-de-mer are world record breakers. Not only are they the largest fruit and seed in the world, but they are also the heaviest.

An average adult walrus weighs about 2,600 lb (1,200 kg), which is a little more than the Atlantic Giant pumpkin.

📊 **FAST FACTS**

Tomatoes are the most popular fruit in the world. 187,000,000 tons (170,000,000 tonnes) were produced in 2016—that's 183 tomatoes for every person on the planet. Bananas are the secondmost popular fruit, with 113,000,000 produced in 2016.

Fantastic **fruit**

The **fruit and vegetables** we buy at the store are not this size. Gardeners grow these **monster fruits** specially to be the biggest, though the world's largest nut is a **natural wonder**.

Border collie dog
This dog breed's usual weight is 37 lb (17 kg), which is about the same weight as a single coco-de-mer seed.

The largest seed
The coco-de-mer tree, which grows only on the Seychelles islands in the Indian Ocean, produces a seed that measures up to 20 in (50 cm) long, which is about the same as a collie dog. The very biggest seeds can weigh up to 55 lb (25 kg) or one and a half collie dogs.

The **coco-de-mer seed** grows inside the biggest wild fruit—it's up to 20 in (50 cm) across.

Flora and fungi data

THERE IS NO SUCH THING AS A **BLACK FLOWER**. EVEN THE **DARKEST OF FLOWERS** ARE JUST **VERY, VERY DARK PURPLE** OR **RED**. THE PIGMENTS THAT GIVE PETALS THEIR COLOR **DON'T PRODUCE BLACK**.

IF THE TREE IS BURNED, THE SMOKE CAN BLIND A PERSON.

THE CARIBBEAN'S **MANCHINEEL TREES** HAVE **WARNING SIGNS** ON THEM NOT TO GO NEAR.

EATING THE APPLELIKE FRUIT CAUSES DEATH BY VOMITING AND DIARRHEA.

THE SAP BURNS THE SKIN. EVEN RAIN DRIPPING THROUGH THE TREE ONTO A PERSON CAN CAUSE BLISTERS.

TOXIC **TREE**

TALLEST **FLOWERS**

Cactus (homegrown):
105.8 ft (32.25 m)—Peruvian apple cactus, India

Cactus (wild):
63 ft (19.2 m)—Cardon, Sonora Desert, Mexico

Sunflower:
30 ft (9.17 m)—Germany

Cactus (homegrown)

Cactus (wild)

Sunflower

PLANTS IN SPACE

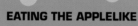

Soviet cosmonauts on the *Salyut 7* space station grew the **first flowers in space**. The plant was *Arabidopsis*, a kind of **rock cress**, which flowered and produced seeds in **zero gravity**.

YEAST FUNGUS, NO MORE THAN **0.4 IN (1 CM) TALL**, EXPLODES AND THROWS ITS **SPORES** UP TO **8.2 FT (250 CM) AWAY**. THAT IS **250 TIMES ITS BODY SIZE**.

FASTEST
FUNGUS

FOR ITS TINY SIZE, THE **HAT THROWER FUNGUS** THROWS ITS SPORES **FARTHER THAN ANY OTHER FUNGUS OR PLANT.**

BIGGEST
LIVING THING
EVER

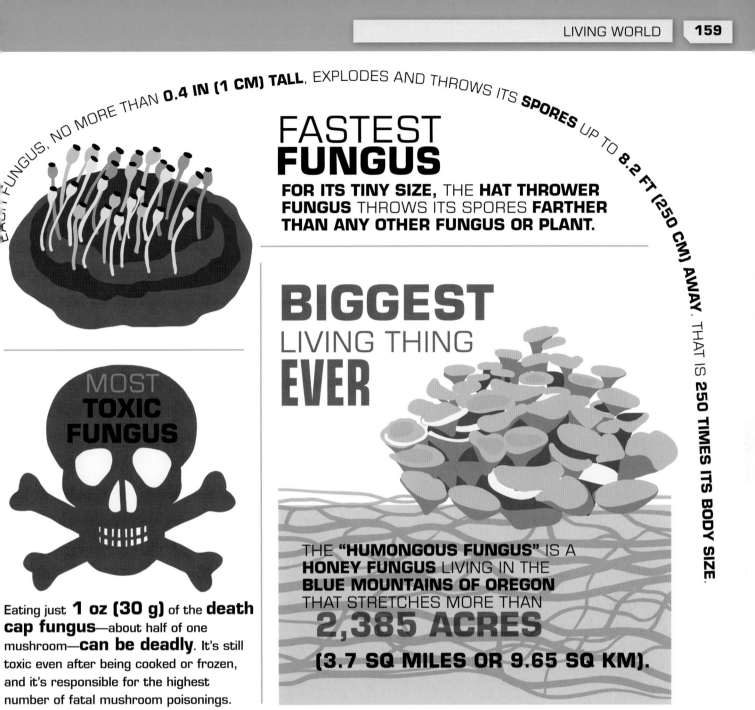

THE **"HUMONGOUS FUNGUS"** IS A **HONEY FUNGUS** LIVING IN THE **BLUE MOUNTAINS OF OREGON** THAT STRETCHES MORE THAN

2,385 ACRES

(3.7 SQ MILES OR 9.65 SQ KM).

MOST
TOXIC FUNGUS

Eating just **1 oz (30 g)** of the **death cap fungus**—about half of one mushroom—**can be deadly**. It's still toxic even after being cooked or frozen, and it's responsible for the highest number of fatal mushroom poisonings.

BIGGEST SINGLE MUSHROOM

The largest fruiting body of a fungus (a mushroom) was discovered in 2010 in China. The brown, woody, rectangular *Fomitiporia ellipsoidea* was 33 in (84 cm) wide, 2 in (5 cm) thick, but 35.6 ft (10.85 m) long—nearly as long as a bus. It weighed about half a ton.

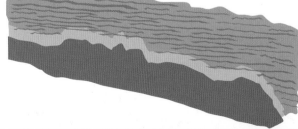

36 FT (11 M) LONG   **35.6 FT (10.85 M) LONG**

Out of this world

Beyond our planet lies infinite space. The vast nature of the Universe means there is always more to explore. Astronauts and astronomers seek new planets, moons, stars, asteroids, and galaxies in the ultimate challenge to discover the biggest, best, and brightest of our cosmos.

A close-up of Buzz Aldrin's bootprint in the lunar soil, taken on July 21, 1969, during the Apollo 11 mission—the first to land on the moon. Earlier in the day, Aldrin's fellow US astronaut Neil Armstrong had become the first man in history to walk on the moon. As he did so, he famously said: "That's one small step for man, one giant leap for mankind."

Space records

In the vast expanse of **outer space**, are things **bigger**, **brighter**, and **colder** than anything experienced on Earth?

Considering the size of the Universe, there ought to be a lot of space records. However, our knowledge of space is limited: we have discovered only a tiny fraction of the Universe. It may be that there are bigger and better things out there. Watch this space!

Dark matter in space can't be seen, but it makes up 24 percent of the mass of the Universe. Visible matter makes up 5 percent. The rest is dark energy.

Biggest-known nebula

Measuring 1,520 light-years across, NGC 604, in the Messier 33 galaxy, is the biggest nebula (cloud of dust and gas). A light-year is the distance light can travel in a year.

Darkest thing

Dark matter is invisible even when you shine a light on it. It has never been seen but is thought to exist because it would explain how parts of the Universe operate.

Brightest thing

In 2013, scientists saw the brightest-ever explosion in space: the death of a star 3.6 billion light-years away. It blasted out gamma rays with 35 billion times more energy than visible light.

Biggest planet

At 599,499 miles (964,800 km) across, HD 100546 b is the biggest-known planet. It has a radius 6.9 times bigger than that of Jupiter and takes 249.2 years to make a single orbit of its star.

📈 FAST FACTS

Telescopes in orbit have shown us most of what we know about space. They detect different kinds of radiation given out by space bodies. The oldest telescope still in use is the Hubble Space Telescope, which detects ultraviolet, visible, and infrared light.

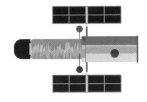

Hubble is 43.5 ft (13.2 m) long—about as big as a school bus.

Launched: April 1990
Location: Low Earth Orbit (340 miles/ 547 km above Earth). Orbits once every 95 minutes at 17,000 mph (27,300 km/h)
Discoveries:
• Age of Universe as 13—14 billion years
• How galaxies form
• Understanding dark energy

Hottest thing
The Universe's hottest stuff is on Earth. An experiment at the Large Hadron Collider, Switzerland, created a temperature that is about 9.5 billion times hotter than the surface of the sun.

Biggest galaxy
Galaxy IC 1101 is 6 million light-years wide (about 50 times bigger than the Milky Way) and may contain 100 trillion stars. It is in the Abell 2029 galaxy cluster, a billion light-years from Earth.

Coldest thing
The boomerang nebula, located 5,000 light-years from Earth, is a chilly −457.9°F (−272.15°C). The nebula expands so quickly, it cools the gas inside.

Oldest galaxy
In 2016, the Hubble Space Telescope discovered the oldest galaxy so far: 13.4-billion-year-old GN-z11. That means it was born about 400 million years after the Big Bang.

Mercury

Smallest planet
At 3,032 miles (4,879 km) across, Mercury is just over one-third the size of Earth.

Least mass
Mercury's mass is 18 times less than Earth's and 5,751 times less than Jupiter, the heaviest planet.

Hottest planet
Although Mercury is nearer the sun, Venus has the highest average surface temperature: 867°F (464°C). Its thick atmosphere traps heat.

Venus

Most volcanoes
Radar has revealed more than 1,600 volcanoes on Venus. No one knows if they are currently active or exactly how many more there are—possibly a million.

📈 FAST FACTS

Earth's iconic features are dwarfed by those on Mars.

Olympus Mons:
13.6 miles (22 km)

Mount Everest:
5.5 miles (8.8 km)

Grand Canyon:
277 miles (446 km)

Valles Marineris: 2,500 miles (4,000 km)

North Polar Basin:
6,600 miles
(10,600 km)

Vredefort crater,
South Africa:
186 miles (300 km)

Densest atmosphere
Made up of 96 percent carbon dioxide, the thick atmosphere on Venus creates a crushing pressure 92 times stronger than that on Earth.

Densest planet
Compared to its size, the amount of material that makes up Earth makes it the densest planet.

What makes a planet unique can depend on its position in our Solar System. For example, Venus is hotter than Mercury because Mercury is *too* near the sun and its atmosphere has burned away. And Earth is the only planet at the ideal distance from the sun to support life—it's neither too hot nor too cold.

Terrestrial planets

Mercury, **Venus**, **Earth**, and **Mars**—known as the terrestrial planets—are all similar in composition, but their **size** and **position** in space gives each one **unique** claims to fame.

Earth

Mars

Earth is the only planet with **life** and to have **liquid water** on its surface.

Largest mountain
Olympus Mons is a volcano that stands 13.6 miles (22 km) above the surface of Mars and is the highest in the Solar System.

Largest crater
The North Polar, or Borealis, Basin covers about 40 percent of Mars. It is not known if it is an impact crater; if so, it would have been caused by an object the size of Pluto.

Largest canyon
Carving a path nearly one-fifth of the way around Mars, Valles Marineris is 2,500 miles (4,000 km) long.

SNAP-HAPPY CURIOSITY

Curiosity is a car-sized rover that was designed to explore Mars as part of NASA's Mars Science Laboratory Mission. Launched on November 26, 2011, it landed on Mars on August 5, 2012, and has continued to perform scientific experiments ever since. The rover holds a unique claim to fame: it took the first-ever selfie on another planet.

Jupiter the giant

Jupiter is the **heavyweight king** of the planets, holding **more records** than any other planet in the Solar System.

Strongest
gravitational pull

The more mass an object has, the stronger its gravitational pull on other objects. Jupiter's gravity is about 2.5 times stronger than Earth's—so if you could jump 39 in (1 m) high on Earth's surface, the same jump would lift you only 15.5 in (39.5 cm) on Jupiter.

Biggest planet

Jupiter measures 88,846 miles (142,984 km) across its widest point (the equator)—that's 11 times the diameter of Earth. Its volume is 343,382,767,518,322 cu miles (1,431,281,810,739,360 cu km), or 1,321 times that of Earth.

Jupiter is the biggest of the gas giants—the four planets made mostly of gas and liquid. All the other planets in the Solar System could fit inside Jupiter, with room to spare!

Fastest **rotation**

Jupiter spins quickly, taking just 9.9 hours to make one complete rotation, even though it is so large. This gives it the shortest day of any planet.

Greatest **escape velocity**

To escape the pull of Jupiter's gravity, a body would need to travel at 37 miles per second (59.5 km per second)—the highest "escape velocity" needed on any planet. Earth's escape velocity is 7 miles per second (11.2 km per second).

Longest **storm**

First observed in 1665, the Great Red Spot is a massive storm that is still raging today. Winds blast an area twice as wide as Earth at speeds of up to 400 mph (644 km/h).

Most **massive**

Being the biggest, it comes as no surprise to find that Jupiter is also the planet with the most mass, weighing in at a huge 4,184,000,000,000,000,000,000,000,000 lb (1,898,000,000,000,000, 000,000,000,000 kg). This planetary powerhouse is 318 times more massive than Earth.

Spots visible on the surface of Jupiter are terrific storms resulting from the planet's fast spin and strong winds.

Brown-and-white-striped bands are swirling gas clouds caused by Jupiter's speedy spin.

The **outer** planets

The three planets farthest from the sun are **Saturn**, **Uranus**, and **Neptune**. These freezing-cold worlds are known as the **gas giants**.

Largest **storm**

Strong winds and violent storms affect the surface of Saturn. The Cassini space probe was the first to detect Dragon Storm, a great storm named after its dragonlike shape.

The rings circling Saturn are made of millions of pieces of ice.

Largest **rings**

Saturn is known for the super-sized rings circling its center. The other gas giants have rings, but they are harder to spot as they contain less material.

Saturn, Uranus, and Neptune are made mainly of helium and hydrogen gas with a small rocky core. Saturn is the second-biggest planet in the Solar System. Neptune is the smallest gas giant, but is still nearly four times bigger than Earth.

Strongest **lightning**

The most powerful lightning strikes occur on Saturn in an area called Storm Alley. The Cassini probe has captured these fabulous flashes on camera.

FAST FACTS

The coldest planets are Uranus and Neptune. Methane gas makes them both look blue.

Uranus

Most rings Uranus has the most rings of any planet, but they are too faint to see.

Only planet to rotate on its side The other planets spin upright, but Uranus was knocked on to its side.

Neptune

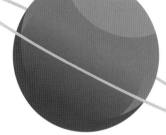

Coldest planet Chilly Neptune has an average temperature of $-353°F$ ($-214°C$).

Strongest winds Neptune has the fastest winds, blowing up to 1,300 mph (2,100 km/h).

Least dense planet

Saturn is the least dense of all the planets in the Solar System. As a result, if Saturn was dropped into water, it would actually float!

Mooning around

A **moon** is a **"natural satellite"**—an object that **orbits** a planet or asteroid. There are **175 known moons** orbiting the **planets** of the Solar System.

Europa

Smoothest moon
Europa is an icy moon with barely any craters. With the exception of a few ridges just a few hundred yards (meters) high, its surface is virtually flat.

Ganymede

Most volcanic activity
Io, Jupiter's third-largest moon, is covered in active volcanoes spewing sulfur into space. Many planets and moons have evidence of past volcanoes, but apart from Earth, the only places with known active volcanoes are moons (Io, Neptune's Triton, and Saturn's Enceladus).

Io

Methone

Smallest moon
At just 3.1 miles (5 km) across, Methone is the smallest-known moon in the Solar System. It orbits Saturn.

Methone is also possibly the least dense moon in the Solar System.

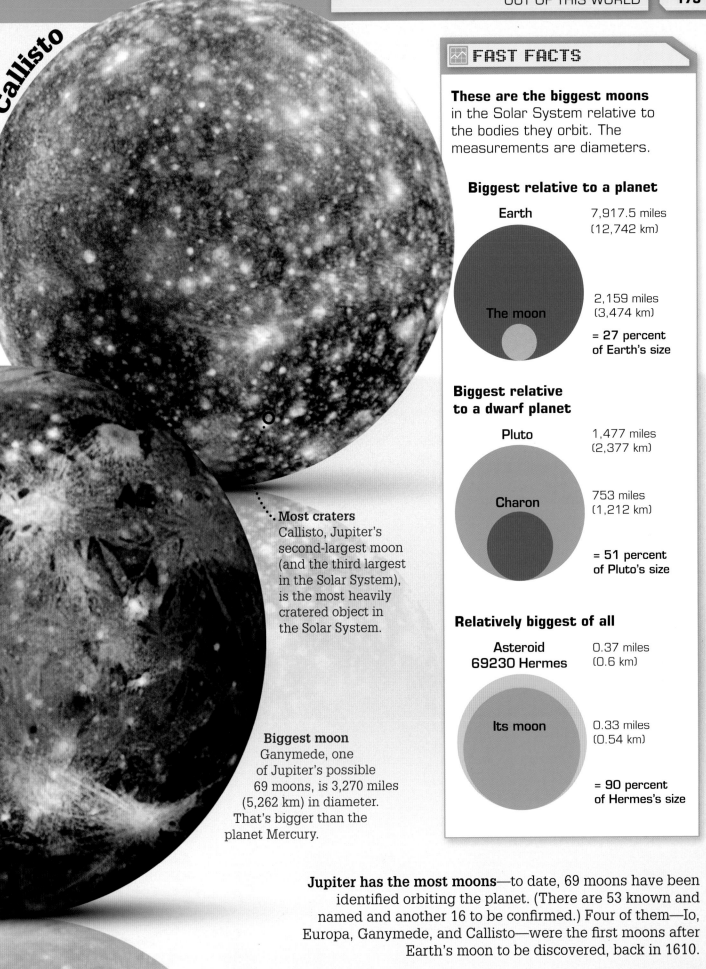

Callisto

FAST FACTS

These are the biggest moons in the Solar System relative to the bodies they orbit. The measurements are diameters.

Biggest relative to a planet

Earth — 7,917.5 miles (12,742 km)

The moon — 2,159 miles (3,474 km)

= 27 percent of Earth's size

Biggest relative to a dwarf planet

Pluto — 1,477 miles (2,377 km)

Charon — 753 miles (1,212 km)

= 51 percent of Pluto's size

Relatively biggest of all

Asteroid 69230 Hermes — 0.37 miles (0.6 km)

Its moon — 0.33 miles (0.54 km)

= 90 percent of Hermes's size

Most craters
Callisto, Jupiter's second-largest moon (and the third largest in the Solar System), is the most heavily cratered object in the Solar System.

Biggest moon
Ganymede, one of Jupiter's possible 69 moons, is 3,270 miles (5,262 km) in diameter. That's bigger than the planet Mercury.

Jupiter has the most moons—to date, 69 moons have been identified orbiting the planet. (There are 53 known and named and another 16 to be confirmed.) Four of them—Io, Europa, Ganymede, and Callisto—were the first moons after Earth's moon to be discovered, back in 1610.

INTERSTELLAR VISITOR

In 2017, astronomers discovered an asteroid approaching the sun on a strange orbit that was eventually confirmed to come from beyond the Solar System. Named "Oumuamua", this strange elongated rock is 1,300 ft (400 m) long and the first interstellar asteroid ever to be identified.

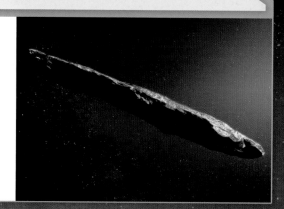

Longest comet tail
Comet Hyakutake has the longest measured tail at 360 million miles (570 million km). It could reach from the sun to beyond the asteroid belt between Mars and Jupiter!

Most disruptive comet
The tail of comet McNaught created such a large disturbance in the solar wind that the probe Ulysses took 18 days to travel through it. By contrast, Ulysses crossed the disturbance created by Hyakutake in just 2.5 days.

The comet **Hale-Bopp** was visible to the naked eye from **May 1996** to **November 1997.**

Biggest comet nucleus
The nucleus (core) of comet Hale-Bopp is estimated to be at least 25 miles (40 km) wide, about 25 times wider than the average comet.

Comets are "dirty snowballs" of snow and gas. Trillions of them lurk at the edge of the Solar System, but we can see and measure them only when they fall toward the sun. Then, as the comets' solid nucleus warms up, they develop a planet-sized atmosphere called a coma, often with long tails of gas and dust streaming behind them in the solar wind of

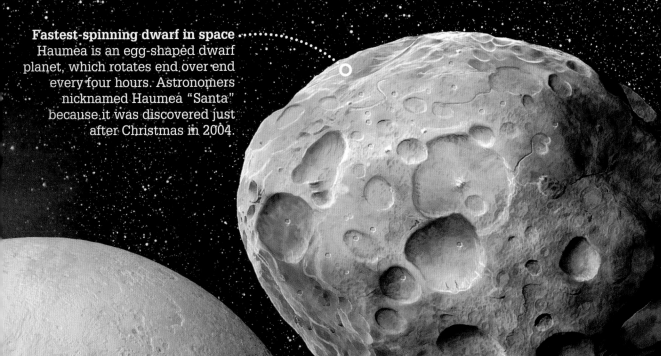

Fastest-spinning dwarf in space
Haumea is an egg-shaped dwarf planet, which rotates end over end every four hours. Astronomers nicknamed Haumea "Santa" because it was discovered just after Christmas in 2004.

Biggest asteroid
The biggest body in the asteroid belt is Ceres. This rocky, cratered asteroid measures 587 miles (945 km) wide and is also classed as a dwarf planet.

First dwarf planet
Pluto was discovered in 1930 and, with a diameter of 1,472 miles (2,376 km), used to be thought of as the ninth and smallest planet. However, it was reclassified as a dwarf planet in 2006.

Space **rocks**

There is more to our Solar System than planets and moons. **Comets**, **asteroids**, and **dwarf planets** can all be spotted whizzing around space.

Space race

From the 1950s to the 1970s, there was a **race** between the **Soviet Union** (now Russia) and the **US** to become the **first nation** to go **into space**. The **Soviets** won.

First man in space

On April 12, 1961, 27-year-old Russian Air Force pilot Yuri Gagarin became the first man in space and the first to orbit Earth, in the rocket *Vostok 1*.

Youngest person in space

Cosmonaut Gherman Titov was 25 when he became the second man in orbit, aboard *Vostok 2* in August 1961.

First woman in space

Cosmonaut Valentina Tereshkova left Earth aboard *Vostok 6* on June 16, 1963. She spent 70 hours in space, orbiting Earth 48 times.

First space walk

Cosmonaut Alexei Leonov made the first EVA (extravehicular activity) on March 18, 1965. It lasted 12 minutes.

Farthest distance from Earth

In 1970, the crew of NASA's *Apollo 13*—Jim Lovell, Fred Haise, and Jack Swigert—reached a record 248,655 miles (400,171 km) away from home.

First space tourist

American businessman Dennis Tito paid $20 million for eight days aboard the ISS in April/May 2001.

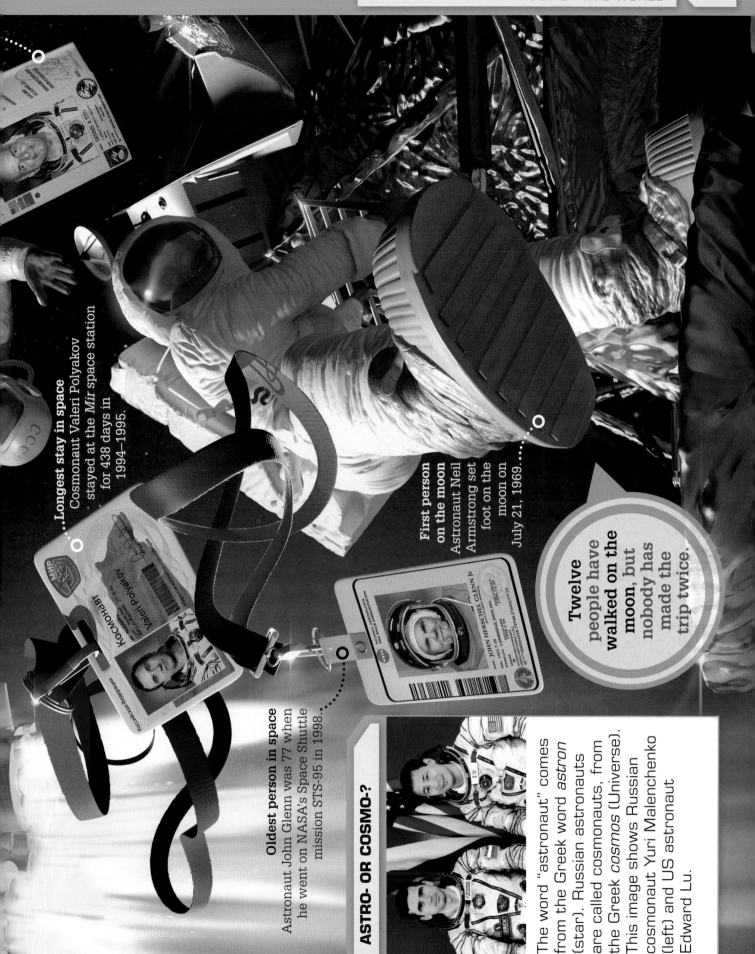

Longest stay in space
Cosmonaut Valeri Polyakov stayed at the *Mir* space station for 438 days in 1994–1995.

First person on the moon
Astronaut Neil Armstrong set foot on the moon on July 21, 1969.

Oldest person in space
Astronaut John Glenn was 77 when he went on NASA's Space Shuttle mission STS-95 in 1998.

Twelve people have walked on the moon, but nobody has made the trip twice.

ASTRO- OR COSMO-?

The word "astronaut" comes from the Greek word *astron* (star). Russian astronauts are called cosmonauts, from the Greek *cosmos* (Universe). This image shows Russian cosmonaut Yuri Malenchenko (left) and US astronaut Edward Lu.

MEN ON THE MOON

On July 21, 1969, as part of the Apollo 11 mission, Neil Armstrong and Buzz Aldrin became the first men to walk on the moon. This is a picture Armstrong took of Aldrin—his reflection is clearly visible in the visor of Aldrin's space helmet. The pair spent around two and a quarter hours on the lunar surface.

Rocketing **ahead**

From **satellites** to **shuttles**, people have sent a lot of **high-tech hardware** into space. But which was the **first** or the **fastest**, and which one traveled the **farthest**?

First artificial satellite
The basketball-sized Russian satellite *Sputnik 1* broadcast radio signals from low Earth orbit for 21 days in 1957.

First manned spacecraft
Spending 108 minutes in space in April 1961, *Vostok 1* made one orbit of Earth with Soviet cosmonaut Yuri Gagarin on board.

Fastest launch speed
In 2006, the *New Horizons* probe, designed to fly by Pluto, made the speediest launch with speeds of 36,373 mph (58,536 kph)—that's more than 9.9 miles (16 km) per second.

First rocket in space
Designed as a weapon during World War II, a German V-2 missile reached an altitude of 109 miles (176 km) during a test launch in 1944.

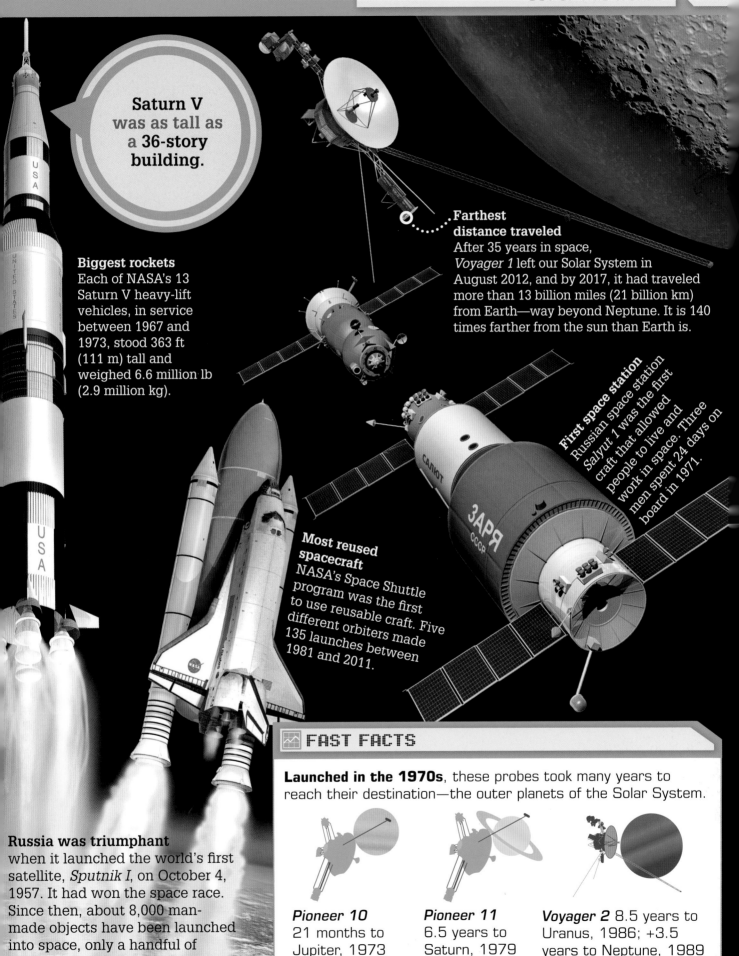

Saturn V was as tall as a 36-story building.

Biggest rockets

Each of NASA's 13 Saturn V heavy-lift vehicles, in service between 1967 and 1973, stood 363 ft (111 m) tall and weighed 6.6 million lb (2.9 million kg).

Farthest distance traveled

After 35 years in space, *Voyager 1* left our Solar System in August 2012, and by 2017, it had traveled more than 13 billion miles (21 billion km) from Earth—way beyond Neptune. It is 140 times farther from the sun than Earth is.

First space station

Russian space station *Salyut 1* was the first craft that allowed people to live and work in space. Three men spent 24 days on board in 1971.

Most reused spacecraft

NASA's Space Shuttle program was the first to use reusable craft. Five different orbiters made 135 launches between 1981 and 2011.

Russia was triumphant

when it launched the world's first satellite, *Sputnik I*, on October 4, 1957. It had won the space race. Since then, about 8,000 man-made objects have been launched into space, only a handful of which have left Earth's orbit.

📈 FAST FACTS

Launched in the 1970s, these probes took many years to reach their destination—the outer planets of the Solar System.

Pioneer 10 21 months to Jupiter, 1973

Pioneer 11 6.5 years to Saturn, 1979

Voyager 2 8.5 years to Uranus, 1986; +3.5 years to Neptune, 1989

Spectacular space station

Since **1998**, the *International Space Station* (**ISS**)—and the **astronauts** aboard it—has been **breaking** a number of **records** in space.

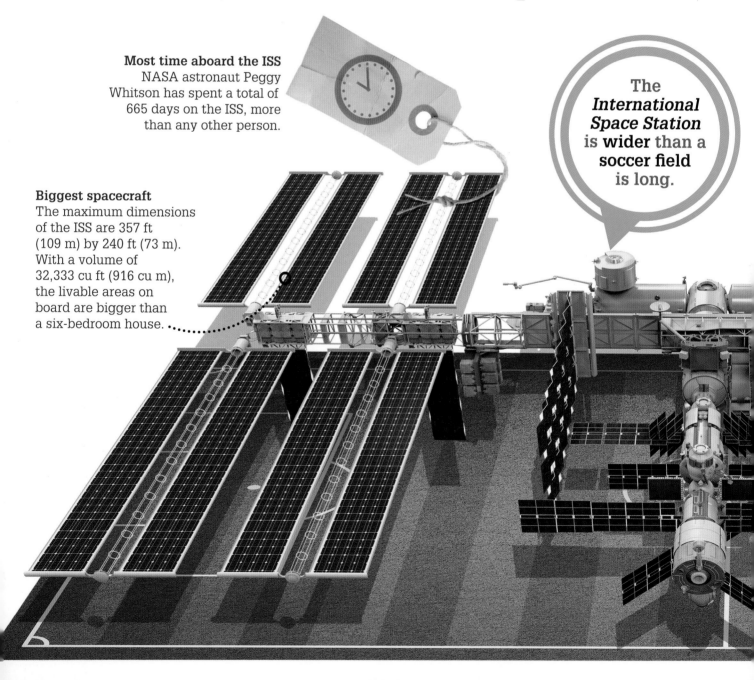

Most time aboard the ISS
NASA astronaut Peggy Whitson has spent a total of 665 days on the ISS, more than any other person.

Biggest spacecraft
The maximum dimensions of the ISS are 357 ft (109 m) by 240 ft (73 m). With a volume of 32,333 cu ft (916 cu m), the livable areas on board are bigger than a six-bedroom house.

The *International Space Station* is **wider** than a soccer field is long.

The first section, or module, of the ISS was launched in November 1998. Two years later, the first astronauts were able to live and work on board. After adding more modules, including science labs, solar arrays, and robotic arms, the building was finished in 2011. But work began again in 2016, with plans to send more modules over the next few years.

FAST FACTS

The first space station, *Salyut 1*, was launched by Russia in 1971. It was not only much smaller than the ISS, but it also spent less time in space—just 175 days. It made 2,929 orbits around Earth, before it was intentionally destroyed.

Length: 65 ft (20 m)
Width: 13 ft (4 m)
Volume: 3,500 cu ft (99 cu m)

Heaviest spacecraft
Including all the modules up to 2011, the ISS weighs 925,335 lb (419,725 kg)—nearly twice as much as *Mir*, which was the next-largest and heaviest space station. The ISS's weight is equivalent to that of 320 cars.

Longest continuously inhabited spacecraft
There have been astronauts at the ISS since November 2000, with new crews coming out to replace returnees. It broke the record for longest continuously inhabited spacecraft back in 2010, when it beat *Mir*'s 3,644 days.

Most science in space
In March 2017, the six-person crew of Expedition 50—made up of one European (ESA), two NASA astronauts, and three Russian cosmonauts—achieved 99 hours of scientific research on the ISS in one week.

Most expensive object ever
With a price tag of more than $114 billion (£80 billion), the ISS is not only the most expensive spacecraft but also the costliest item ever built, both on Earth and in space.

GIANT TELESCOPE

The world's biggest optical telescope is Gran Telescopio Canarias (GTC) in Tenerife, Canary Islands, Spain. It has a 34-ft- (10.4-m-) wide aperture (opening) and 36 mirrored panels to focus visible light from space.

During its trial run **FAST** detected **two pulsars** (spinning neutron stars).

The FAST dish is covered in 4,450 triangular aluminum panels, which can be tilted in different directions by computer.

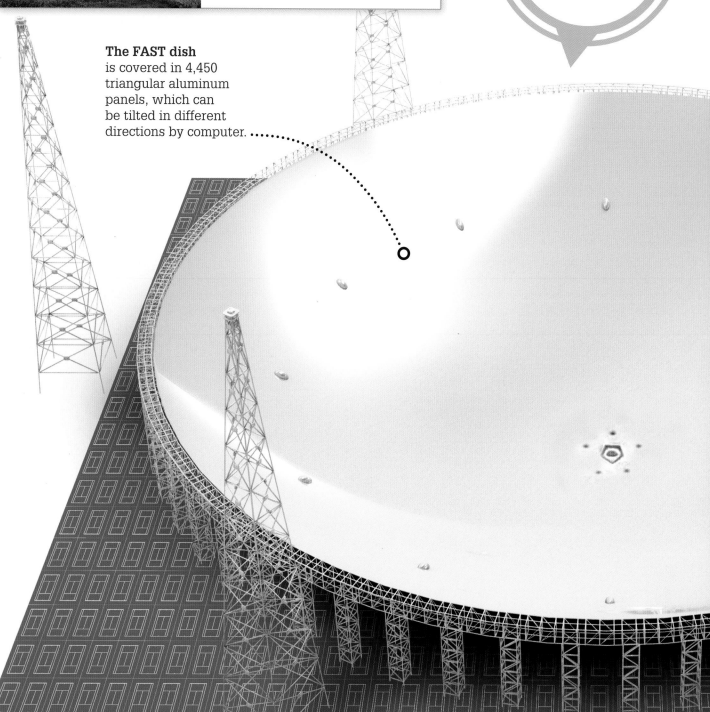

The biggest dish

The **world's biggest telescope** is the Five-hundred-meter Aperture Spherical Telescope (**FAST**) in China. As the name suggests, the dish measures an incredible **500 m** (1,640 ft) across.

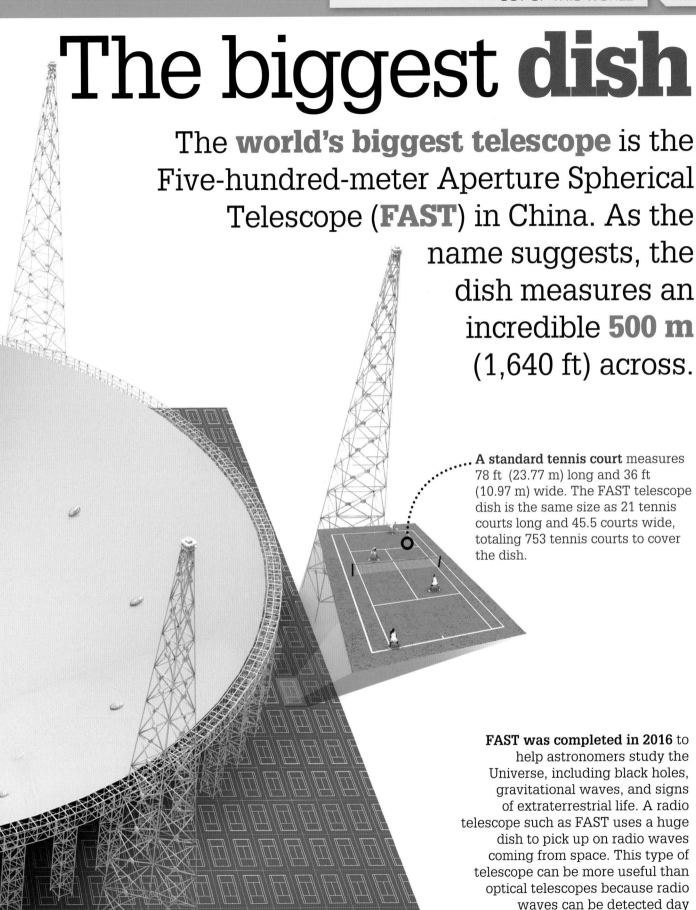

A standard tennis court measures 78 ft (23.77 m) long and 36 ft (10.97 m) wide. The FAST telescope dish is the same size as 21 tennis courts long and 45.5 courts wide, totaling 753 tennis courts to cover the dish.

FAST was completed in 2016 to help astronomers study the Universe, including black holes, gravitational waves, and signs of extraterrestrial life. A radio telescope such as FAST uses a huge dish to pick up on radio waves coming from space. This type of telescope can be more useful than optical telescopes because radio waves can be detected day or night in any weather.

Space data

BIG BUILD

The biggest thing in the Universe is the **Hercules-Corona Borealis Great Wall**. It's not a physical wall but a probable galaxy supercluster of stars an average of

6–10 billion light-years across

and which contains billions of galaxies.

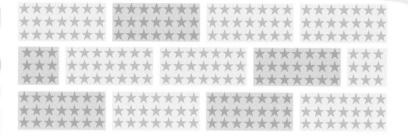

SPACE WALKS

12 MINUTES—DURATION OF FIRST SPACE WALK (ALEXEI LEONOV, 1965)

8 HOURS, 56 MINUTES—LONGEST SPACE WALK (JIM VOSS AND SUSAN HELMS, 2001). THAT'S MORE THAN **44 TIMES** LONGER.

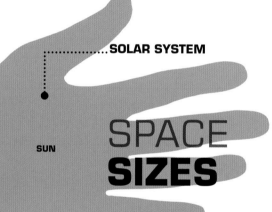

···· **SOLAR SYSTEM**

SUN

SPACE SIZES

If the **SOLAR SYSTEM** could shrink to fit in the palm of your hand, **the SUN** would be smaller than **a grain of sand**. On the same scale, **the MILKY WAY** would be the **size of North America**.

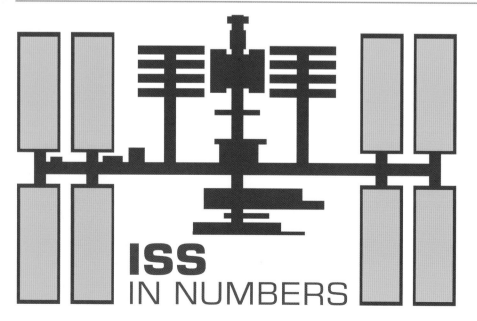

ISS IN NUMBERS

8 MILES (12.9 KM)
OF ELECTRICAL WIRING ON BOARD

52 COMPUTERS
CONTROL THE **ISS SYSTEMS**

42 FLIGHTS
TO BUILD **THE ISS**

27,000 SQ FT
(2,500 SQ M)
OF SOLAR PANELS PROVIDE POWER

PLANETARY TIME

MERCURY HAS THE LONGEST DAY, EQUAL TO 176 EARTH DAYS.

JUPITER HAS THE SHORTEST DAY, **9 HOURS** AND **56 MINUTES** LONG.

NEPTUNE HAS THE LONGEST YEAR, TAKING **164.8 EARTH YEARS** TO ORBIT ONCE AROUND THE SUN.

MERCURY HAS THE SHORTEST YEAR OF ALL THE PLANETS, **87.9 DAYS**.

87.9 DAYS

PASSPORT TO THE PLANETS

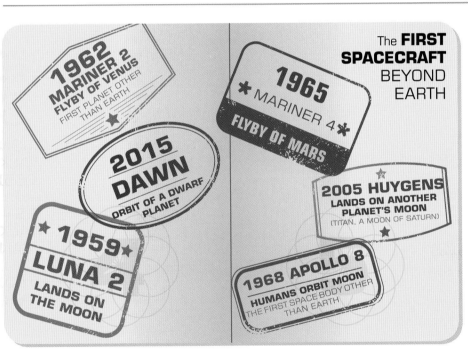

1962 MARINER 2 FLYBY OF VENUS — FIRST PLANET OTHER THAN EARTH

2015 DAWN ORBIT OF A DWARF PLANET

1959 LUNA 2 LANDS ON THE MOON

The **FIRST SPACECRAFT** BEYOND EARTH

1965 MARINER 4 FLYBY OF MARS

2005 HUYGENS LANDS ON ANOTHER PLANET'S MOON (TITAN, A MOON OF SATURN)

1968 APOLLO 8 HUMANS ORBIT MOON — THE FIRST SPACE BODY OTHER THAN EARTH

SPEED IN SPACE

THE FASTEST **A HUMAN** HAS EVER **TRAVELED IS**

24,791 mph (39,897 km/h)

THIS WAS EXPERIENCED BY **THE CREW** OF **APOLLO** 10 ON THEIR WAY BACK TO **EARTH** FROM **ORBITING THE MOON** IN 1969.

MEMORABLE MOONS

ENCELADUS

MIRANDA

NESO

PHOBOS

The **MOST REFLECTIVE** body in space, reflecting more than **90 per cent** of the energy it receives from **sunlight**.

Home to the **BIGGEST CLIFF** in the **Solar System**. Verona Rupes is thought to be **3–6 miles (5–10 KM)** tall.

The most **DISTANT MOON** from its planet, orbiting an average **30.8 million miles** (49.5 million km) from Neptune.

The **CLOSEST MOON** to its planet, **3,700 miles** (5,980 km) above **MARS**—66 **times closer** than our moon to Earth.

INDEX

ACKNOWLEDGMENTS

Dorling Kindersley would like to thank: Andrea Mills for editorial assistance; Hazel Beynon for proofreading; and Helen Peters for the index.

The publisher would like to thank the following for their kind permission to reproduce their photographs:

(Key: a – above; b – below/bottom; c – center; f – far; l – left; r – right; t – top)

4 Alamy Stock Photo: CNP Collection (crb); Xinhua (cla). **Depositphotos Inc:** CogentMarketing (crb/Frame). **Dreamstime.com:** Michael Drager (crb/Throne). **Getty Images:** Antonio Scorza / AFP (cra). **Rex by Shutterstock:** Sipa Press (ca). **5 Getty Images:** Anna Shtraus Photography (tl); Joel Sartore (tc). **NASA:** (tr); JPL / DLR (br). **6 Alamy Stock Photo:** Xinhua. **8 Dreamstime.com:** Dita Nemcova (cr). **9 Alamy Stock Photo:** Jeffrey Miller (cb); Navapon Plodprong (cra). **Dreamstime.com:** Genadijs Zelenkovecs (cla). **Getty Images:** Subhendu Sarkar / LightRocket (ca). **Science Photo Library:** Sputnik (clb). **11 Getty Images:** d3sign (tr). **12-13 Getty Images:** Ansonmiao. **18-19 TurboSquid:** Alex_BY (cb); everlite (Rubble B). **18 Alamy Stock Photo:** Cultura Creative (RF) (clb). **19 TurboSquid:** 3degestar (cl). **20 Alamy Stock Photo:** Stephen Barnes (l). **Depositphotos Inc:** lkpro (r); Nyker (c). **21 Alamy Stock Photo:** Juniors Bildarchiv GmbH (r). **Depositphotos Inc:** Goinyk (l). **22-23 Getty Images:** Buena Vista Images. **27 123RF.com:** Dmytro Nikitin (c). **28 Getty Images:** NASA / Earth Observatory / Handout / Corbis (clb). **34 Rex by Shutterstock:** Sipa Press. **36 Alamy Stock Photo:** CNP Collection (cra); DPA picture alliance (cla); Newsphoto (crb). **Depositphotos Inc:** CogentMarketing (Frame). **Dreamstime.com:** Michael Drager (Throne). **Getty**

Images: Dubber / ullstein bild (c). **37 Alamy Stock Photo:** Icelandic photo agency (cr). **Depositphotos Inc:** Albund (Podium). **Getty Images:** Murali / Pix Inc. / The LIFE Images Collection (ca); Jorge Rey (cla). **38 Alamy Stock Photo:** AF archive (c); Glasshouse Images (clb); Pictorial Press Ltd (cb). **38-39 Depositphotos Inc:** Mayakova (Popcorn); TitoOnz (Background). **39 Alamy Stock Photo:** AF archive (cl, c); Pictorial Press Ltd (cla); Photo 12 (ca); Robertharding (clb). **45 Getty Images:** Jeff Pachoud / AFP (tr). **46-47 Royal Geographical Society:** Alfred Gregory. **49 Alamy Stock Photo:** Marka (tl). **50 Alamy Stock Photo:** Granger Historical Picture Archive (cl). **Getty Images:** Bettmann (clb); Mondadori Portfolio (tc); Universal History Archive / UIG (tr). **50-51 Alamy Stock Photo:** Antiqua Print Gallery. **Depositphotos Inc:** PicsFive (Background). **51 Getty Images:** Alexander Sentsov / ITAR-TASS (cb); US Navy / The LIFE Images Collection (c). **52 Alamy Stock Photo:** Paul Fearn (cr); Interfoto (cb). **Getty Images:** Bettmann (tr). **52-53 Alamy Stock Photo:** Antiqua Print Gallery (Map). **Depositphotos Inc:** PicsFive (Background). **53 Getty Images:** Corbis (tl); Hulton-Deutsch Collection / Corbis (tr); Mark McDonald / MCT (crb). **54-55 Dreamstime.com:** Daniel Domański (Background); Feng Yu (Paper). **55 Alamy Stock Photo:** Chris Hellier (crb); WENN UK (cla). **Depositphotos Inc:** PicsFive (t); Stillfx (cr). **Dreamstime.com:** Axstokes (br); Photka. **56 Getty Images:** Antonio Scorza / AFP. **58 Alamy Stock Photo:** Everett Collection Historical (ca). **60 Alamy Stock Photo:** Action Plus Sports Images (cra). **63 Alamy Stock Photo:** Aflo Co., Ltd. (bc). **64-65 TurboSquid:** onurozgen. **65 Getty Images:** Bettmann (br). **66 Getty Images:** Vincenzo Pinto / AFP

(clb); Mark Thompson (cla); Bettmann (ca); ISC Images & Archives (cb). **70 Getty Images:** Bettmann (clb). **72 Getty Images:** Andy Lyons (clb). **73 Getty Images:** Ian Walton (crb). **75 Dreamstime.com:** Jerry Coli (cl). **Getty Images:** Bill Frakes / Sports Illustrated (c). **76-77 Getty Images:** Cameron Spencer. **80 Getty Images:** AFP (cra). **80-81 Getty Images:** Bettmann. **82 Getty Images:** Anna Shtraus Photography. **85 Getty Images:** Bettmann (cra). **87 Alamy Stock Photo:** Granger Historical Picture Archive (crb). **90 Alamy Stock Photo:** WENN Ltd (bl). **92-93 TurboSquid:** Juan Montero. **93 123RF.com:** jvdwolf (tr). **Dorling Kindersley:** National Motor Museum Beaulieu (tl). **Dreamstime.com:** Typhoonski (ftl); Alex Zarubin (tc). **Getty Images:** Michael Cole / Corbis (ftr). **94-95 Getty Images:** China Photos. **100-101 Getty Images:** NY Daily News Archive. **102-103 Getty Images:** Richard Juilliart / AFP. **104 Alamy Stock Photo:** NASA Image Collection (clb). **104-105 Alamy Stock Photo:** Agencja Fotograficzna Caro. **106 Depositphotos Inc:** Sepavone (cb). **Dreamstime.com:** Martin Kemp / Martink (crb). **107 Depositphotos Inc:** Richie0703 (crb). **iStockphoto.com:** undefined undefined (cla); x-drew (cra). **108-109 Getty Images:** STR / AFP. **114 Getty Images:** Joel Sartore. **122-123 FLPA:** Martin Willis / Minden Pictures. **124 Alamy Stock Photo:** Elizabeth Masoner (cla). **137 Getty Images:** Patrick Dykstra / Barcroft Images / Barcroft Media (ca). **138 Dorling Kindersley:** Jerry Young (bl). **Dreamstime.com:** Isselee (tr); Studioloco (c). **139 Alamy Stock Photo:** Sabena Jane Blackbird (bc). **Dorling Kindersley:** E.J. Peiker (c). **Dreamstime.com:** Werayut Nueathong (cr). **144-145 Heyuan Dinosaur Museum. 148-149 Getty Images:** Mark Widhalm / Field Museum Library. **160 NASA. 162 ESA /**

Hubble: Hui Yang (University of Illinois) and NASA (cra); NASA (cb); NASA and the Hubble Heritage Team (STScI / AURA) (bc). **NASA:** ESO / L. Calçada (crb); Goddard Space Flight Center (clb). **162-163 Depositphotos Inc:** Colors06. **163 ESA / Hubble:** NASA and the Hubble Heritage Team (STScI / AURA) (fclb, cr/NGC 2174); NASA and The Hubble Heritage Team STScI / AURA (clb). **Getty Images:** Harald Ritsch / Science Photo Library (cl). **NASA:** ESA, Hubble Heritage Team (STScI / AURA) (cr); ESA, P. Oesch (Yale University), G. Brammer (STScI), P. van Dokkum (Yale University), and G. Illingworth (University of California, Santa Cruz) (crb). **164 NASA:** Johns Hopkins University Applied Physics Laboratory / Carnegie Institution of Washington (tl); JPL (c). **164-165 NASA:** NOAA / GOES Project (c). **165 NASA:** HQ (br). **166-167 NASA:** JPL-Caltech / MSSS. **168-169 NASA:** JPL-Caltech / SwRI / MSSS / Kevin M. Gill (b). **170-171 NASA:** ESA and Erich Karkoschka (University of Arizona) (c). **172-173 NASA:** JPL / DLR (cb). **172 NASA:** Cassini Imaging Team, ISS, JPL, ESA (cb); JPL / DLR (bl, c). **173 NASA:** JPL / DLR(German Aerospace Center) (tl). **174-175 NASA:** JHUAPL / SwRI (c). **174 ESO:** (tc). **NASA:** (cl); European Southern Observatory (c); ESA / JPL-Caltech (ca); E. Slawik (b). **175 Alamy Stock Photo:** Science Photo Library (tr). **NASA:** JPL-Caltech / UCLA / MPS / DLR / IDA (crb). **177 Alamy Stock Photo:** SPUTNIK (bc). **178-179 NASA. 182-183 Alamy Stock Photo:** Nerthuz (cb). **Depositphotos Inc:** Andrey_Kuzmin (b). **Dreamstime.com:** Luminis (Tag). **184 Dreamstime.com:** Inge Hogenbijl (tl)

All other images © Dorling Kindersley

For further information see: www.dkimages.com